One Body One Spirit

Principles of Successful Multiracial Churches

By

George A. Yancey

16

EasyRead Large

RHYW

Copyright Page from the Original Book

InterVarsity Press
P.O. Box 1400, Downers Grove, IL 60515-1426
World Wide Web: www.ivpress.com
E-mail: email@ivpress.com

InterVarsity Press® is the book-publishing division of InterVarsity Christian Fellowship/USA®, a student movement active on campus at hundreds of universities, colleges and schools of nursing in the United States of America, and a member movement of the International Fellowship of Evangelical Students. For information about local and regional activities, write Public Relations Dept., InterVarsity Christian Fellowship/USA, 6400 Schroeder Rd., P.O. Box 7895, Madison, WI 53707-7895, or visit the IVCF website at <www.intervarsity.org>.

All Scripture quotations, unless otherwise indicated, are taken from the Holy Bible, New International Version®. NIV®. Copyright ©1973, 1978, 1984 by International Bible Society. Used by permission of Zondervan Publishing House. All rights reserved.

Cover design: Cindy Kiple
Cover image: Digital Vision/Getty Images

ISBN 978-0-8308-3226-2

Printed in the United States of America ∞

Library of Congress Cataloging-in-Publication Data

Yancey, George A., 1962-
   One body, one spirit: principles of successful multiracial churches / George A. Yancey.
     p. cm.
Includes bibliographical references.
  ISBN 0-8308-3226-2 (pbk.: alk. paper)
  1. Race relations——Religious aspects——Christianity. 2. Church work
with minorities——United States. I. Title
  BT734.2 .Y365 2003
  259'.089—dc21

                                                   2003008232

P	21	20	19	18	17	16	15	14	13	12	11	10	9	8	7	6	5	4
Y	22	21	20	19	18	17	16	15	14	13	12	11	10	09	08	07			

TABLE OF CONTENTS

"My heart soared with gratitude and renewed hope for the church's future as I read *One Body, One Spirit.* George Yancey's compelling call to build multiracial worshiping communities is healing, motivating and, with the aid of his insights, realizable. This practical guide ushers us toward the heavenly worship that awaits."

SUNDEE TUCKER FRAZIER,
author of *Check All That Apply: Finding Wholeness as a Multiracial Person*

"I thoroughly enjoyed reading George Yancey's new book, *One Body, One Spirit.* I find this work to be extremely scholarly, helpful and inspiring. This book is a must for anyone who is interested in starting a multiracial ministry or concerned about race relations in the church. I have known George for a number of years and seen his love for Christ and his dedication to the touchy issues of racial reconciliation. *One Body, One Spirit* will be a welcome resource for anyone who has made the courageous decision to go on this journey."

KATHY H. DUDLEY,
Board Chair and Founder, Dallas Leadership Foundation

This book is dedicated to those who have defied our society's false barriers of race in the past, to those who defy them today, and to those who will continue to do so in the future.

FOREWORD

I see God working on the hearts of people everywhere I travel. More and more people want to join God in his desire for multiracial congregations. Always, the questions are the same: How can we become a multiracial church? What does it take? What should we focus on? What changes should we make? We are multiracial, but how can we maintain our racial mix, and how can we grow in our faith and relationships together? The desire is there, but the knowledge is not.

This desire-knowledge gap is what makes this book so important and so special. George Yancey has written a remarkable book that makes a groundbreaking contribution. Drawing extensively on the first-ever national study of multiracial congregations, he uncovers seven main factors that these congregations have in common. He takes us through these commonalities, step by step, in an engaging and easy-to-read manner. Contained in the book is the very heart of what it takes to transform one's church into a multiracial congregation, and what it takes to develop together once a church is demographically multiracial.

As I read through this book, I grew more amazed at how much knowledge is contained in its pages. For example, earlier in the book, Yancey addresses an assumption held for at least the last thirty years: that churches filled with people of the same race grow fastest. So entrenched is this assumption in contemporary Christianity that no one has ever bothered to actually test it to see if it is true. Yancey does test this assumption, and his finding has the potential to turn our understanding of church growth on its head.

What is most impressive is that this significant finding is just one part of one chapter. Chapter after chapter is packed with useful information. Yet despite so much vital information in this book, Yancey's gift for communicating through stories made me want to keep turning the pages, never feeling overwhelmed by the material. Yancey has a gift for communicating complex ideas in such a smooth and interesting manner that they do not seem complex. He makes learning interesting! He spent many months in multiracial congregations around the country and their stories are presented here. So every point in the book is not only drawn from the churches but is illustrated with real churches and real people.

I know Yancey's heart, and it is that this book will be a service to you as you follow God's leading. Read the book, in prayer follow its advice, and watch God work!

Michael O. Emerson
Founding Director of the Center on Race, Religion and
 Urban Life Rice University

ACKNOWLEDGMENTS

This book would not have been possible without God's faithfulness and the contributions of several individuals. First and foremost I thank the staff at InterVarsity Press for supporting the vision of this book. I especially thank Al Hsu, who has been invaluable in helping to see me through this process. While I have published Christian material in the past, Al's suggestions were critical in helping me make this work a ministry instead of just a writing project.

I am also grateful for the support of the Lilly Endowment, Inc. and grant #1998-1384-000, which supplied the academic support necessary to allow me to gain these results. In addition to those at Lilly who foresaw the vision of this work I am eternally thankful for the help of my co-researchers Dr. Michael Emerson and Dr. Karen Chai who labored with me to design and implement this important project. Michael, as the principal researcher of the grant, has been especially helpful in encouraging me to do this book and taking the lead in securing the grant. Without him I do not think there would have been this grant, and this book would not have been possible.

I benefited greatly from several readers of this material. I am thankful for Dr. Fred Prinzing and Dr. Charles Ware for early readings of this work. I am also thankful for Arturo Lucero, Hank Hankerson, Dr.

Marc Erickson, William Emanuel and Roger Grothe for their comments on later versions of this manuscript. Curtiss DeYoung also helped me find valuable information that contributed greatly to this book. I thank the pastors, priests, church leaders and others that we interviewed for this project and those we interviewed in the pretesting stage of this work. To protect their confidentiality I will not identify them, but without their input it would be impossible to learn the lessons this book has to offer.

Finally, I thank my wife, Sherelyn, who supports me in our day-today lives. She was a big help by interviewing some of the respondents and by offering valuable advice at different stages of this project. I also thank her for putting up with me as I put in long hours on this project, as well as for her example as a racial reconciler.

1

INTRODUCTION

Soon after accepting my present academic position, my wife and I began searching for a church. We had just moved to Fort Worth, and finding a church in a place where you have never lived before is often difficult. Being married complicates the task, as you must combine the interests and needs of two individuals instead of one. We found a church relatively close to our home. That church had many fine qualities that we both wanted: friendly individuals, a dynamic pastor, and solid theology. But I was uncomfortable because almost no individuals of color attended the church. I had joined predominantly white churches before, but I am at a point in my life where I want to be in a church containing a reasonable number of racial minorities.

My wife started attending a women's Bible study. Many of the church leaders attended this Bible study. She relayed my concerns—that the church was practically all white—to some of the women in that study. The reaction of the women was quite predictable. They maintained that they were not prejudiced and that their church was quite open to people of all races. They stated that anyone was welcome, including people of other races. They simply could not understand why racial minorities did not come to their church.

I had met many of these women. They were right when they said that they welcomed me, an African American. I sensed no racial bigotry in any of the members of that church. Yet I also knew that African Americans were not, in large numbers, going to join this church at any point in the near future. The reason why this church was going to remain predominantly white for the conceivable future was not because the church leadership intentionally barred racial minorities. Rather, it was due to the inability of this church, like most American churches, to create multiracial Christian environments.

It is a common belief that Sunday morning is the most segregated time of the week. Unfortunately, this is still the case in America. Whereas we have seen the number of integrated schools and workplaces increase,[1] it is unclear whether there has been any increase of integrated churches. If multiracial churches are desirable, then we clearly have not done a good job in creating integrated religious institutions. Yet many Christians who desire to create multiracial churches are at a loss for how to go about doing so. They are not unlike my wife's friends who wonder why people of other groups do not attend their church even though they are very willing to accept people of other races as new church members.

The question of my wife's friends continues to haunt our churches in America. How do we guide those who truly want to racially diversify their congregations? The main focus of this book is to provide principles that will enable a church to become multiracial or to help a multiracial church maintain its racial diversity. Each church has unique factors that can either inhibit or encourage mixtures of races. For this reason I have chosen to present general principles that can be adjusted for a particular church rather than try to offer specific advice for all potential and actual multiracial churches.

DEFINING MULTIRACIAL CONGREGATIONS

Before I discuss the creation and maintenance of multiracial churches it is first important to define the term "multiracial church." Clearly a church of one thousand whites with an Asian American does not have the same type of racial mixture as one that has three hundred Asian Americans. In defining a multiracial church it is important to assess the percentage of people who are a different race than the majority racial group in the church. However, there are also issues of culture and ethnicity that must be taken into account in the definition as well.

4

It is important for me to address these issues as I explore what a multiracial church is.

For the purpose of this book I will define a multiracial church as a church in which no one racial group makes up more than 80 percent of the attendees of at least one of the major worship services. If we define multiracial churches in this way, then only 8 percent of all American churches are multiracial.[2] This standard means that a church can be multiracial even if four out of every five individuals in that church are of the same race. If we demand a more rigorous definition of racial diversity, then even this 8 percent estimate of multiracial churches is too high. While there are scholarly reasons to believe that even this small percentage of members from different races is enough to change the racial atmosphere of the church,[3] it can also be argued that churches with such a high percentage of members of the same race are not multiracial. Yet, for the purpose of this book, I will define multiracial churches with this 80 percent criterion, even if some may disagree with this definition, since there is sociological evidence that such churches differ from monoracial churches.[4]

Even though only 8 percent of all churches have a worship service in which no more than 80 percent of the attendees are of a given race, in a higher percentage of churches the actual membership of the church is racially diverse. This occurs because missions or outreach programs bring in members of different racial groups (e.g., outreaches to immigrant groups or inner city ministries), but those individuals worship at a different time or place than the main body of the church. These churches have a main worship service made up of members of a given race and separate worship services for other races. For example, in graduate school I was a member of a predominantly white church that had a mission outreach to an African population in our city and a mission outreach to Hispanic Americans in the neighborhood. Yet these two groups did not regularly worship with the main body of the church.

In one sense this may be considered a multiracial church, as distinct racial groups learn how to work together in the same building. However, there is little social interaction between the different racial groups. This church had few functions where all three of the racial populations of the church were encouraged to attend—and those events were considered novelties, not opportunities to develop long-lasting friendships. Such a church simply does not experience many of the benefits and challenges of multiracial ministry. I believe that the difficult task faced by Christian leaders today is to create real multiracial fellowship, rather than merely learning how to share a church building with members of another racial group. So for the purpose of this book, I will also define multiracial churches as those where members of different racial groups attend the same worship service.

While ethnicity is a concept that is similar to race, there are important distinctions that have to be acknowledged. Generally, ethnicity refers to groups that have cultural distinctions, while race is used to denote groups that are perceived to be physically different from each other. When we talk about those with contrasting ethnicities we are looking at the distinctions between Puerto Ricans and Mexicans, Germans and Swedish, Japanese and Chinese. Most Americans, for example, do not perceive the two groups in each of the previous pairs to be physically different from each other, but rather to have distinct cultures from each other. On the other hand, racial differences are based on the perception that groups have physical differences. When we talk about blacks and whites, we are talking about groups that most Americans perceive as physically different from each other.[5]

Ethnicity can be a very important factor in examining social divisions. It might be argued that multiethnic is a better term to use than multiracial. Multiethnicity also has a sounder scriptural basis since different ethnic, but not racial, groups are discussed in the Bible. The concept of race and racism itself is relatively new in human history, and so multiracial congregations are not discussed in the Scriptures, although there are examples of multiethnic ones (e.g., Jews and Gentiles worshiping together). Multiethnic congregations of that time likely engendered the same types of difficulties as multiracial congregations face today. Thus, by concentrating on the idea of multiracial congregations, a concept that is not in the Scriptures, I am touching upon the same issues that must have come up with the multiethnic churches that are discussed in the Scriptures.

In this book I will concentrate on multiracial churches instead of multiethnic ones. With one exception, the churches I have studied were not merely multiethnic, but also contained different racial combinations. I argue that in our society racial differences carry more social significance than ethnic differences. While ethnicity can be a barrier to understanding between members of diverse groups, especially if we are dealing with first-generation immigrants, usually racial distinctions create the most problems in our society. Thus, a German-Swedish church generally has far fewer problems to contend with than a black-white church. To examine how Christians can overcome the most intense social barriers, we must look towards multiracial, rather than just multiethnic, churches. While there are tremendous challenges for attracting first-generation immigrants, who are most likely to focus on ethnic differences rather than racial distinctions, my contention is that the greater problem lies in overcoming racial barriers in the United States, and that there has been lax motivation to inspire congregations to resolve racial alienation. My prayer is that this resource will open our hearts to facilitate racial healing for Jesus' sake.

I also want to make clear that I will not be using the term *multicultural* when I describe these churches. It is true that most of the churches in the Lilly study can be correctly described as multicultural since contrasting racial groups tend to bring distinct cultures into the congregation. But the term *multicultural* has been used to enunciate dimensions such as gender, age, sexual preference, and regional differences. Given the comprehensive way that the concept of multiculturalism is commonly used, I believe that it is too vague a term to use for describing the type of churches I explored. Therefore, *multicultural* is not as accurate as is the term *multiracial* when describing these churches.

Finally, when I discuss multiracial congregations I am not limiting my discussion to just black-white churches. Many people think about race relations as just a black and white issue, but multiracial churches can include any combination of different racial groups in our society. The multiracial churches I have studied contain some combination of whites, blacks, Latinos or Asians.[6] In fact the multiracial churches were more likely to be white and either Latino or Asian than to be white and black.

THE LILLY STUDY OF MULTIRACIAL CHURCHES

I learned much about multiracial churches through my travels over the past two years. As a co-researcher of a major sociological project[7] I was blessed with an opportunity to learn about multiracial churches firsthand. Our multiracial congregational project was sponsored by a grant by the Lilly Endowment. Dr. Michael Emerson and Dr. Karen Chai were co-researchers in the project. They are both committed Christians who are devoted to both conducting solid research and serving Christ. Michael Emerson, the principal researcher, is writing an academic book that is based on this data. The task I have chosen for myself is to present a more accessible, practical book on the principles of multiracial church growth for Christian leaders who are interested in maintaining or starting a multiracial ministry.

As researchers, we wanted to explore the social scientific questions that surround multiracial churches. As Christians, we wanted to know if multiracial Christianity was truly possible in an America where racial alienation is commonplace. The answer is *yes*—but only with hard work. Again and again I saw successful multiracial churches. These churches did not happen by accident. In the following pages I hope to document examples of some of the hard work that created these multiracial ministries and to provide tools for those who wish to engage in such labor. By doing so I hope to create a book for pastors and church leaders who want insight into creating or sustaining racially integrated congregations. This book will give some valuable principles that they can adapt to their own particular settings.

To accomplish this purpose I use the results of the Lilly research project and my own personal experience in interacting with multiracial ministries to investigate these principles. There were four major steps to this research. First, we conducted a national telephone survey that targeted individuals who went to multiracial churches as potential respondents. Second, we sent out a questionnaire that was completed by the leaders of multiracial churches. Third, we went to several cities in the United States and interviewed pastors and attendees of multiracial congregations. During each of these three steps, we also included individuals who attend monoracial churches, and monoracial churches themselves, so that we would have a group of individuals or churches to compare to our multiracial attendees or churches. Fourth, I sent a short follow-up questionnaire to churches that had been previously identified as multiracial. This questionnaire basically asked about the characteristics of multiracial churches. More information about the methodology of this study is contained in appendix A.

Finally, I want to note that this is not an academic book. I have intentionally avoided the academic jargon and theory that so often makes it difficult for social scientists to communicate with those who could otherwise benefit from our work. To help me enunciate answers for Christians who wish to engage in multiracial ministry, a purely academic treatment of this topic is not the best way to present the material. I chose to use a less technical writing style that reaches a broader audience. However, I have used the endnotes to document some of the statistical findings that I gathered in the data and that substantiate many of the claims I make in the book.[8] If you are not interested in exploring some of the methodological ways I developed my conclusions and are only interested in a practical presentation of these findings, then feel free to ignore those notes.

Chapter two will explore the past and present reality of multiracial churches in our society. In chapter three I will examine the question of whether multiracial churches are desirable in America. In chapter four I will explore the different types of multiracial churches that exist. Chapter five contains a brief summary of the general principles that help to determine the level of success that multiracial churches enjoy. Chapters six through twelve explore these principles and demonstrate examples I discovered in the multiracial churches that we have researched over the past two years. In the last chapter I will conclude with a few final important issues and with special attention given to the topic of attracting African Americans into multiracial congregations.

2

MULTIRACIAL CHURCHES: PAST AND PRESENT

Racism is a relatively new phenomenon in human history.[1] Motivations for oppression in ancient societies did not revolve around the perception of racial or biological differences between various people groups; rather, oppression was based on one culture conquering another culture. Yet while racism is a relatively recent phenomenon in human history, it has been a staple of the cultural diet in the United States. The very birth of our nation was made possible by racist justifications that led to the annihilation of Native American tribes, and this nation has historically exploited the labor of African, Hispanic and Asian Americans.

It is fair to ask whether multiracial churches can be created in the racially charged climate that characterizes our nation today. To answer that question it is valuable to examine the history of multiracial churches in the United States. By doing so we will learn that multiracial churches have existed in our society, despite the level of racism that has historically dominated the United States. Understanding the effects of this historical racism is important for us to be able to

14

understand some of the obstacles that hinder the growth of multiracial churches. It is not an accident that racial alienation is a part of our society. This alienation is the natural result of our history of racial abuse.

BRIEF HISTORY OF MULTIRACIAL CHURCHES

We have always had multiracial congregations, even though these churches have been few and far between.[2] For example, early American indentured servants were both blacks and whites. They shared roughly the same status in society. As such, multiracial congregations of black and white indentured servants were not uncommon. Of course, much of this changed as the system of American slavery moved from one of indentured servanthood to one of slavery for life. Yet there is evidence of slaves attending predominantly white churches[3] although it was a situation of segregation and oppression.

After the Civil War, Southern hostility towards African Americans served to reinforce congregational segregation. In the North segregation was not enforced as much through formal laws as it was through social customs.[4] As a result of Southern laws and Northern practices, a 1930 study by the Federal Council of Churches indicated that few blacks were allowed to participate in predominantly white churches.[5] A later study indicated that in the 1940s there were no white churches open to African Americans unless the neighborhood surrounding the church was at least black by majority.

However, by the later part of the 1900s a few multiracial churches began to gain notoriety. The Church of the Fellowship of All Peoples in San Francisco was one of these congregations. It remained multiracial throughout its entire history. It was intentionally formed to be multiracial and helped inspire other efforts at multiracial ministry. Furthermore, Clarence Jordan pioneered an interracial community in southern Georgia called "Koinonia Farm." This community had a powerful influence on Millard Fuller, the founder of Habitat for Humanity.[6] Jordan conceptualized the racial tensions present during the 1960s as analogous to the biblical hostility between Jews and Samaritans.[7] Efforts such as his indicated a weak but growing movement among Christians to deal with racial segregation through the development of multiracial ministries for blacks and whites.

The propensity for congregational integration is somewhat different for nonblack racial minorities. Hispanic and Asian Americans are racial groups that have a large percentage of immigrants. First-generation immigrants are unlikely to attend integrated churches because they have a strong need to maintain the culture of their native countries. Often the worship services of these churches are conducted in their native tongue instead of English. Some evidence indicates that second-generation Asian Americans immigrants prefer English-speaking services but still desire churches made up of individuals of their own race.[8] To the degree that these nonblack minority groups are able to integrate into the dominant culture they are more likely to attend churches with whites. However, research has suggested that only racial minorities with higher income and educational status are able to experience such integration.[9]

Despite these problems, multiracial churches have existed throughout our country's history and continue to exist today. Their witness gives us hope that racial barriers can be breached and Americans may someday be able to enjoy a multiracial Christian environment. The historical reality of multiracial churches allows us to hope that we can create racially integrated congregations in a country that today is less overtly racist. But to create them we have to be realistic about the racial problems that continue to plague our society and that make the creation and sustenance of multiracial churches problematic.

THE PRESENT REALITY

A significant hindrance to the development of multiracial churches is the degree of racial alienation present in the United States. Generally, most racial minorities understand that this alienation exists, while many whites do not perceive how severe racial hostility still is in the United States. To appreciate the task of creating multiracial churches and assess whether it is desirable to undergo the effort needed to establish these churches, we must understand the depth of our racial divide.

Many Americans wish that we could have a colorblind society. In such an ideal society we would be blind to the importance of skin color in our society. Many individuals believe that acting as if we are a colorblind society is the best way to produce a race-neutral society. They assert that we should ignore racial differences to the same degree that we ignore differences in hair or eye color.

But this notion of "colorblindness" discounts the degree of racial alienation we have in our society. We simply cannot treat skin color like we treat hair or eye color. Skin color represents a history of racial oppression and disenfranchisement that cannot be ignored. We have never had neighborhoods segregated by hair or eye color. There is no history of Americans systematically enslaving or murdering individuals based on their hair/eye color. Hair/eye color is not used to "profile" individuals and label them as criminal suspects. We can be very colorblind when it comes to hair or eye color because there is no history of discrimination, nor evidence of contemporary racism, based upon those qualities. Skin color, and other attributes we link to racial groups, is linked to historical and contemporary evidence of racism. When Christians forget this fact and believe that we have a colorblind society, they can believe that multiracial churches will naturally develop once we eliminate overt racial prejudice.

I understand the desire for a colorblind society. Colorblindness as it pertains to racial issues is a laudable goal since it would denote a complete lack of racial prejudice. Perhaps one day we can have a colorblind society. But in today's world so-called colorblindness is a denial of the fact that racial identity continues to play an important role in our lives. For many racial minorities the notion of colorblindness becomes a barrier to racial justice since it denies the reality of racism and prejudice that they face.[10] Because colorblindness discounts the importance of race, it allows people like my wife's friends to remain confused about why racial minorities are not eager to join predominantly white churches. Many white Americans believe that because we have relative political and legal racial equality, there is no reason for racial minorities to feel alienated. They contend that focusing on historical racism is counterproductive to positive race relations. Let me illustrate why I do not agree with such a position.

Many, if not most, Americans live in homes that they own. These homes were built upon land that was once controlled by Native Americans. How did the land once belonging to Native Americans end up being owned by other Americans, most of whom are not Native Americans? We know that Native Americans have historically been robbed of their land by a variety of means. They were lied to and driven off their land. They were forced into treaties that they did not want to sign. If they did not sign them then they were murdered or starved to death on reservations. Even when they did sign them, the United States government generally broke the treaties. The list of atrocities goes on. The land that Americans have gained to build their homes was not gained through an equitable transaction, but by intimidation and genocide. Americans who own homes today have indirectly gained by the historical oppression of Native Americans. They can buy their homes at a much cheaper price because the land had long ago been stolen from American Indians. To a relatively lesser extent, European Americans today have also gained from the slavery of African Americans, from the disempowerment of Hispanic Americans and from the racism suffered by Asian Americans.

I am not ignoring the responsibilities that racial minorities have for their own economic/social situation, but rather I am illustrating that what has happened to those racial groups historically does have a contemporary racial effect. White Americans have benefited, and continue to benefit, from past racism. For example, African Americans in the past were not allowed to purchased homes in wealthier, predominantly white neighborhoods, even if they had the money to afford such homes. Because of this housing discrimination, blacks were concentrated into the slums of the inner city. This segregation allowed whites to channel economic and educational resources away from black neighborhoods, which in turn helped European Americans benefit at the expense of African Americans. Even though today the sort of legal and violent sanctions that prevented blacks from leaving the inner cities may not be used, blacks still find it difficult to leave the slums that their parents and grandparents were forced to endure. These slums trap blacks since they do not offer educational or occupational opportunities that whites in the suburbs enjoy. In this sense, African Americans today are still paying for the historical discrimination past generations faced.[11]

The ideology of colorblindness fails to take into account these historical effects since this philosophy ignores the social dimension of race. A philosophy of colorblindness denies that historical racism and the effects that have been suffered by people of color are real. As such, this philosophy fails to serve people of color. This is why people of color often find it difficult to have meaningful dialogue with European

Americans who unflinchingly hold to a colorblind perspective.

If the effects of racism were merely historical, that would be damaging enough. Unfortunately, racism continues to affect racial minorities today. The recent concern over racial profiling is a case in point. Racial profiling is the practice of police officers investigating racial minorities to a greater extent than they investigate white Americans. The most commonly used example of profiling is that on certain highways police officers are more likely to pull African American drivers over than drivers of other racial groups.[12] Yet there is no evidence that black drivers are any more likely to break traffic laws than other Americans. This tendency for African Americans to be pulled over is likely due to the prejudice and stereotypes that blacks face on a regular basis. Because African Americans are more likely to be perceived drug dealers or gangsters, they are pulled over more often than other Americans.

This higher level of suspicion faced by African Americans is more than mere inconvenience or embarrassment. Because they are more likely to be suspected, black criminals are more likely to be caught than white criminals. This distorted propensity contributes to an image of blacks as criminals. The general public, seeing the high number of black criminals who are caught, concludes that the stereotype of the black criminal is correct. This can lead to increased police suspicion, and more African American—rather than European American—criminals are arrested. This type of vicious circle is called a self-fulfilling prophecy, and it helps explain how racist stereotypes lead to unequal outcomes for racial minorities.

Many other excellent sources provide examples of how racial minorities suffer from prejudice and discrimination today.[13] These occurrences illustrate that racial divisions in our society are not based upon illusions. Rather, these divisions are based upon real racial problems that exist in our society and have germinated over a long period of time. Only after we realize the extent of the racial strife that exists in the United States, and realize that this strife will not easily disappear, can we appreciate the difficulty of developing multiracial congregations.

The problem of creating a multiracial ministry is exacerbated by the fact that it is in churches where we find some of the closest friends we will ever have. It may be easier to develop a multiracial workplace or school since we are not expected to "have fellowship" with anyone who attends our schools or places of employment. But as Christians we understand that it is important to accept members of our church as "our brothers and sisters in Christ." Thus, it is in our churches that racial alienation may provide the most powerful barrier to the creation of a multiracial atmosphere. A person may have a diverse workplace and attend an integrated school even if that person does not trust individuals of other races. The desire for money or education can overcome the racial distrust such a person may have. Yet few individuals with a high level of racial distrust will attend a multiracial church where one must look upon members of other races as equals. To overcome the racial barriers in our churches we will have to deal honestly with the racial demons that have invaded our society.

CONCLUSION

There is good and bad news that emerges from this historical examination of multiracial congregations and contemporary race relations. The bad news is based on the fact that all relationships are built on past encounters. For example, if I lie to my friends then they will eventually learn not to trust my statements. In time my lying will affect how they treat me. Even when I tell the truth I cannot expect my friends to believe me because the lying has created barriers to trust between my friends and myself. Likewise, our racist past has created barriers to racial understanding in our society. Even when whites intend to help people of color, many racial minorities are often hesitant to trust and work with whites because their previous experience with whites has proven to be fruitless. To underestimate racial barriers leads to the kind of confusion the white women in my wife's Bible study experienced. Racial mistrust hinders the creation of multiracial churches. Those who want to develop multiracial churches are wise to acknowledge the difficulty that lies in establishing them.

But the good news is that this difficulty is not the entire story of our racialized history. Multiracial churches have existed in our society, despite the racial oppression and exploitation of people of color. Their historical existence proves that we can overcome the racial barriers that work against their creation today. God is bigger than the racial sins that divide us if we just allow him to guide us and if we are willing to work hard at overcoming racial alienation. It is difficult to learn from the multiracial churches of the past. But thanks to the Lilly study we can now learn from contemporary racially integrated congregations so that we will be able to overcome these barriers.

3

SHOULD WE HAVE MULTIRACIAL CHURCHES?

Since multiracial churches do not naturally spring up, it will take a significant amount of effort to create and sustain them. Given the level of effort needed, and because there are so many important tasks for churches to undertake, it should be asked whether attempts to create multiracial congregations are justified or just wasted energy. Furthermore, there are those who argue that multiracial churches are undesirable in and of themselves. Even if multiracial churches were not difficult to achieve, such individuals would maintain that we still should not attempt to create integrated religious institutions. Their concerns must be heard and answered by those of us who want to develop multiracial churches. In this chapter I will make the argument that multiracial churches are desirable and worth the effort it takes to create them while also answering the concerns of those who oppose such efforts.

ARE MULTIRACIAL CHURCHES DESIRABLE?

Some individuals have argued that multiracial churches are not desirable, no matter how much or little effort it takes to create them. There are two major arguments that support this position: a church growth paradigm and a cultural pluralism argument.

Some Christians argue that church growth is one of the most important tasks of the church. Proponents of the church growth school argue that to accomplish growth it is vital to create churches where potential members of that church are comfortable and will eventually join the church.[1] One of the ways of developing this comfort level is to target certain subcultures. If churches are designed to minister to individuals within certain subcultures, then those individuals will find themselves in congregations where members share their lifestyles and experiences. Therefore, if we want to reach people who live in suburbs, then we need churches filled with suburban-ites; to reach the Generation X crowd, we need churches filled with Gen Xers and so on.[2]

Since this church growth paradigm emphasizes the creation of a monocultural environment, multiracial churches can be a problem. Race is clearly a factor that helps define American subcultures. Multiracial churches, by their very nature, contain many different subcultures, and because of this mix of subcultures, some church growth experts fear that racially integrated churches will not grow due to their members' different lifestyles and experiences. These differences create the theoretical possibility of conflict and an atmosphere that is uncomfortable for new church attendees. Church growth experts argue that to spend energy putting together a church of many different racial groups detracts from the church's main duty—to win as many souls as possible.

On the other hand, cultural pluralism questions the value of integration itself. They argue that in the rush to integrate members of multiple races we will allow the power of the dominant race to overwhelm the integrity of minority cultures. For example, historically there have been attempts to "integrate" Native Americans into the dominant culture. One such attempt involved the use of boarding schools. Native American children were sent to these boarding schools to separate them from their own culture. They were not allowed to speak their native language, wear their native clothes, have long hair or practice their religion. These regulations were in accordance with the philosophy of "kill the Indian and save the man."[3] Advocates for racial minorities argue that this philosophy denigrates the culture of Native Americans and implies that European American culture is superior. They perceive assimilation as a further extension of white superiority. This philosophy of cultural pluralism mandates that the cultures of minority groups are to be respected and maintained in as pure a form as possible. Its proponents argue that the value of racial minority cultures is equal to the value of European American culture and to force racial minorities to accept a Eurocentric Christianity is sin.

Since the church is an important center of the culture of many racial minority groups, cultural pluralists are generally skeptical of multiracial churches. Much of the work of these scholars does not directly condemn multiracial churches, but instead advocates a type of cultural, racial purity that excludes the development of multiracial ministries. For example, William Cenkner edited a book in which several Catholic theologians develop a multiculturalist position about the value of different cultures and their independent contributions to the larger Catholic Church.[4] Likewise, within Protestant denominations, the development of black theology[5] has supported the idea of maintaining distinct African American congregations and liberation theology[6] has supported the value of maintaining the uniqueness of Latino American congregations. Such theologies regard preventing the loss of black and Latino culture as a priority for minority Christians. While cultural pluralists may not directly attack the worth of multiracial churches, their desire for multiracial churches is low since such churches may lead to the assimilation of minority cultures by the majority group.

Both the church growth advocates and proponents of cultural pluralism raise legitimate concerns about multiracial churches. I do not believe that church growth should be the only purpose of the church, but adding members to one's church is a worthy goal. Assessing whether racial integration allows us to reach people, or hinders our ability to reach out, is a task that must be taken seriously. Cultural pluralists are correct when they point out that racial minorities have suffered from attempts to blindly assimilate them into the dominant culture. If multiracial churches merely represent another attempt to smother the culture of minority group members, then I should reconsider my support of them.

But while the church growth and cultural pluralism perspectives are valid critiques of multiracial church-es, I still contend that multiracial churches have much to offer. Indeed, I argue that these churches are vital for our faith and our witness.

CHURCH GROWTH ARGUMENTS

Is it the case that multiracial churches are less likely to grow and more likely to have interpersonal conflict than monoracial churches? Advocates of the homoge-neous church growth principle contend that the inabil-ity of multiracial churches to offer a common racial culture to the members of that church inhibits the ability of these churches to grow. Multiracial churches are forced to incorporate different racial cultures, which can mean that multiracial churches have less of an ability to present the gospel of Christ in a culturally relevant way to members of certain subcultures.

For example, if we are attempting to reach a community of Chinese immigrants, we will want to create a worship environment that is respectful of the Chinese culture. This will take a church that is sensitive to the needs of these immigrants and attempts to meet those needs. This church will likely have services in Mandarin, help immigrants with issues such as citizenship and operating in the American capitalist system, as well as construct a worship service that reflects elements of Chinese culture. Chinese immigrants would get a chance to see the gospel of Christ reflected in a culturally appropriate way. A multiracial church is not likely to have the emphasis on Chinese culture that a predominately Chinese church can have since a multiracial church has to be mindful of cultural aspects from many different racial/ethnic groups. A multiracial church would not be able to reflect the gospel to the Chinese immigrants in a culturally appropriate way. Advocates of church growth contend that a multiracial church would be unable to reach out to Chinese immigrants in as effective a manner as a church specifically designed to meet their needs.

This example illustrates the best case church growth experts have for monoracial churches. This is perhaps the situation that lends itself to the strongest possible church growth argument for monoracial churches. There are some situations, such as ministry to first-generation immigrants, where monoracial churches or ministries can be the best way to go. To advocate for multiracial churches is not to believe that all churches can or should be multiracial.

However, developing a monoracial church is not the only way one may envision church growth. An emphasis on monoracial church development assumes that Americans define themselves totally by their racial identity. While racial identity is very important to most minority Americans, it is not the only way we identify ourselves. There are other powerful ways by which Americans create their social identities. If we follow the logic of the church growth specialist, then we also need churches of only Democrats or Republicans, rich or poor, suburbanites or city dwellers, sports enthusiasts or fine arts lovers, computer nerds or nature lovers, fans of westerns or science fiction. No church can create a culture in which one is totally comfortable. There are going to be cultural differences in all large groups of individuals. So even if the church growth advocates are correct, every church still must decide which aspects of culture they want to build their church around and in which aspects of culture there will be diversity. In such a manner multiracial churches can be built around cultural aspects other than race, and they can theoretically enjoy just as much growth as monoracial churches.

Do monoracial churches grow faster? The church growth school claims that a racially homogeneous atmosphere serves to create a cultural climate that encourages people of a certain racial group to join a congregation. Historically, Americans were much more likely to grow up in a monoracial environment. But as the number of racial minorities has grown in our society, younger Americans have experienced more residential, occupational and educational racial integration than their parents and grandparents. Thus, Americans who have been socialized with only members of their own race are becoming less common. Given this tendency we are seeing more Americans who are comfortable with people of other races. Americans today, unlike their parents and grandparents, have experienced the influences of many different racial cultures. The modern civil rights movement and the lessening of overt racial hostility have led to more egalitarian and intimate interracial contact among Americans today. Therefore, we now have more people who are much more comfortable interacting with members of different races and are more likely to enjoy a religious environment that is multiracial.

My wife is a great example of such a person. She grew up in northern Idaho—about as white a part of the United States as you can have. With the exception of Native Americans from a close reservation, she had little exposure to people of color. After receiving her bachelor's degree she became a registered nurse and moved to San Antonio, Texas. There she was exposed to a city where whites were a numerical minority and encountered a Hispanic culture that she did not experience in Idaho. She met a number of Africans and African Americans (eventually marrying one). Her social networks now also include Asian Americans and mixed-race Americans as well. Her reaction to her racially diverse lifestyle is one of excitement, not of dread. While her closest friends still tend to come from the long-term relationships she developed with whites in the Pacific Northwest, she now has many good friends of different races. She also has a racially diverse taste in music, art and food. Her personal preference is not for the all-white environment in which she grew up but for her current multiracial atmosphere. She is not unlike many Americans who have adapted to, and even thrived in, the new multiracial social environment.

While the church growth school argues that the comfort of a homogeneous racial atmosphere is conducive to church growth, the growing presence of Americans who are comfortable with people of all races suggests that it is monoracial—not multiracial—churches that may struggle to grow. It is in the multiracial churches that people like my wife feel the most comfortable. Her desire for racial diversity makes the atmosphere of multiracial churches more "comfortable" to her than the atmosphere of monoracial churches. If creating a comfortable environment is what is important to church growth, then multiracial churches are better suited for twenty-first-century Americans than monoracial churches. If my theory is correct, then multiracial churches should be more likely to grow than monoracial churches.

Until now those who are concerned with the effects of a racially diverse congregation on church growth could only speculate about whether such diversity would have a dampening effect upon potential church growth. But with the data from the mailout survey in the Lilly study it is now possible to see whether monoracial churches are more likely to grow than multiracial churches. One of the questions in the survey asked if their church has grown over the past twelve months. From the questionnaire I found that multiracial churches are more likely to have grown over the past year than monoracial churches (66.1 percent multiracial churches have grown versus 57.1 percent of monoracial churches have grown). So for the first time it can clearly be said that there is no evidence that monoracial churches grow faster than multiracial churches.

It is possible that factors other than the racial makeup of these churches account for this difference. For example, it might be the case that multiracial churches are smaller than monoracial churches. A statistician will tell you that if you start out with a smaller group, then higher percentages of growth are more likely to occur simply because of your lower starting point.[7] But the evidence of the Lilly study reveals that multiracial churches are actually larger than monoracial churches.[8] This data also indicates that multiracial congregations are on average thirty years younger than other congregations, and it can be argued that this accounts for the higher rate of growth. However, even when I controlled for the founding date of the church I still found that multiracial congregations are more likely to grow than monoracial churches.[9]

This evidence shows that the church growth argument is flawed. Churches that are not based on a single racial culture are more likely to grow than monoracial churches, probably through their ability to attract Americans who are very comfortable with multiracial social settings. These churches are not hampered by the difficulties of dealing with different cultures. Their growth illustrates that multiracial churches may be the churches that best represent our emerging American society. As more Americans begin to live out a multiracial lifestyle (working in integrated workplaces, interracially marrying, attending interracial schools), I expect that the advantages multiracial churches have over monoracial churches in terms of church growth will simply increase.

It might be argued that I have overstated the number of people who are comfortable with multiracial settings. But since multiracial churches are just as, or even more, likely to grow than monoracial churches, such a critique does not hold up to empirical analysis. The growth of multiracial churches indicates that there is a growing, emerging market for multiracial ministries. Furthermore, as the percentage of European Americans decreases in the coming decades we will see more interracial interactions and thus more individuals who are comfortable with multiracial religious environments.[10] The multiracial church is the church for the future in the United States.

Is there more conflict in multiracial churches?
Yet even if multiracial churches are as likely to grow as monoracial churches, what about the possibility that the multiracial nature of these churches will lead to more conflict? After all, what good is it for multiracial churches to grow rapidly if they are less stable than monoracial churches and will soon split? Racial diversity brings the potential of another source of conflict. If a multiracial atmosphere brings a higher tendency for interpersonal conflict, then

it can be suggested that Christians are better off without multiracial churches.

The data in the mail survey asked the respondents about whether there have been disagreements in their churches. They were asked to indicate how much disagreement had developed over the past two years on eight difficult issues: theology, money/budget, worship style, programs/missions, decisions of the church, clergy leadership, clergy behaviors and member behaviors. While racial/cultural issues were not included as a possible source of disagreement, it does seem likely that if there is racial hostility within a church that this hostility would spill over into one of these areas that was listed. For example, a white-black church might have conflicts about whether a Eurocentric or black gospel style of worship music might be utilized in the church service. Conflicts over worship styles are the stuff of church splits as they represent which type of culture is going to dominate the church.[11]

Yet in only one of these eight issues were members in multiracial churches significantly more likely to have disagreements than monoracial churches.[12] On the other seven issues the difference between multiracial and monoracial church was too small to be statistically measured. If there is a racial conflict that can be reflected in these issues, the Lilly data was not able to consistently capture it. It appears that multiracial churches are no more likely to experience conflict than monoracial churches.

It is possible that conflict over racial and cultural issues may play themselves out in issues that were not captured in these eight areas. This unmeasured conflict might eventually cause a church split. The respondents were also asked if the congregation had undergone a church split in the last ten years in hopes of seeing if there is an underlying tendency for those in multiracial congregations to eventually split apart. But once again multiracial churches were not significantly more likely to have undergone such a split than monoracial churches. Concerns about the instability of multiracial churches, relative to monoracial churches, are not supported by empirical data.

I have looked at the reasons why the church growth people might believe that there is more conflict in multiracial churches. But evidence of higher conflict was not discovered. I believe that those who attend multiracial churches are willing to accept the premise of a multiracial atmosphere. Where there is racial or cultural conflict these individuals are willing to work out the problems they face. These conflicts are not seen as being so insurmountable as to create church splits or, as we saw in the last section, a higher than normal loss of members. I speculate that racially integrated churches are just as stable as monoracial churches because they are just as committed to practicing multiracial Christianity as those in monoracial churches are committed to maintaining the racial culture of their church.

THE CONCERNS OF CULTURAL PLURALISTS

I am sensitive to the concerns racial minorities have about maintaining their culture and quick to acknowledge that the way Christianity has been practiced has often done more to affirm European American culture than the majesty of Christ. Given these concerns, any steps toward Christian interracial interaction must be done in a way to assure racial minorities that they will not be called to merely adhere to European American culture. If multiracial churches become a mechanism by which the values within racial minority cultures are eradicated, while no demands are made upon European Americans, then such churches may become the boarding schools of the twenty-first century. Cultural pluralists are rightly concerned that multiracial churches may engage in the same type of mentality that led to the "kill the Indian and save the man" attitude.

But like the concerns of the church growth specialist, the apprehensions of those advocating cultural pluralism were not found when I examined contemporary multiracial congregations. With rare exceptions, multiracial churches generally are not merely Eurocentric churches that have somehow managed to attract racial minorities. For the most part racial minorities do not go to churches that totally ignore their cultural concerns. Multiracial churches that tend to be successful are churches that attempt to meet the needs of members of all races. In this way multiracial churches are not simply bastions of European American culture, but tend to be a mixture of different racial cultures.[13]

Even if multiracial churches allow for the mixing of different racial cultures and do not merely reinforce Eurocentric values, cultural pluralists still have concerns about the threat to racial minorities' cultures. Whether racial minorities lose their cultural values because they have adopted the values of European Americans or whether they lose them because a mixture of several different cultures has usurped those values, a cultural pluralist can still argue that those values are lost nonetheless. The question that must be addressed is whether the maintenance of cultural purity by racial minorities is more important than the possible gains derived from multiracial churches. I argue that cultural maintenance is not more important than these potential gains for several reasons.

First, I challenge the static notion of culture purity. Cultural pluralists assume that the cultures of racial minorities do not change. But all cultures change.

Even before the boarding schools, the culture of Native Americans had undergone tremendous changes due to the influence of European Americans. But Native American cultures also underwent changes even before the European discovery of the "New World." Technical innovations, social revolutions and other agents of change had already had a great influence on American Indians before the coming of Europeans. The same can be said for Africans, Asians and other people of color around the world. Europeans and European Americans exacerbated the social change of these cultures, but their encounter with Europeans was not the only source of social changes for these people groups.

Because cultures of all different races constantly undergo social change, it is a mistake to believe that there is a pristine Native American or Latino American culture that must be preserved against all external influences. All cultures are constantly changing over time and will change regardless of how little or great of an influence they experience from exposure to other cultures. I argue that it is not wise to fight off all possible changes that different cultures may experience. The real concern is whether the changes that cultures have undergone are beneficial or harmful. Many of the effects upon racial minorities by Europeans and European Americans have been harmful, and cultural pluralists are right to be wary of adapting a Christianity that is too Eurocentric. But there is also a danger of taking this justified caution and using it to resist all social changes, including those that can be beneficial.

This leads to a second concern I have with the arguments of cultural pluralists—the emphasis they place on cultural maintenance. All human cultures have both strengths and weaknesses. One of the main sins of the boarding schools was that European Americans ignored the weaknesses of their own culture and the strengths of Native American cultures. In doing so they embarked on a plan to eradicate Native American cultures. There are strengths within European American cultures that can benefit Native Americans. But for American Indians to truly benefit from these strengths we must have an attitude of acceptance whereby the European Americans can also benefit from the strengths found among Native people.

The arrogance of European Americans who discounted the values in the cultures of other races is obvious in the example of the boarding school. What is less obvious is that cultural pluralists are making a similar assertion when they suggest that minority cultures must be preserved regardless of the cost. This assertion is based on the assumption that minority group members cannot learn from white Americans. But since the cultures of members of all races are made up of human beings corrupted by sin, it is foolish to believe that there is any human-created social culture that cannot be improved. A healthier attitude toward interaction with other cultures is to learn from our cultural interaction rather than adopt a bunker mentality by which we attempt to maintain our cultural purity. This learning is more likely within multiracial churches than same-race churches.

Finally, proponents of pluralism often fail to recognize that influence does not flow in one direction. Their fear is that only racial minorities will have to change to accommodate white Americans. Yet interracial interaction gives racial minorities an opportunity to influence majority group members as well. In fact, I have conducted research that suggests that whites who attend churches where blacks also attend are more likely to have sympathetic attitudes toward the social and political interests of blacks than whites who attend churches where there are no blacks.[14] Any good sociologist will tell you that correlation does not necessarily mean causation, and so this difference in attitudes may not be due to the interaction that whites and blacks have in those churches. It is possible that this research merely documents the fact that whites who are more racially tolerant are more likely to attend a church that is multiracial than other whites. Nevertheless, it is not unreasonable to argue that an environment may develop within multiracial churches where racial understanding can emerge and whites are exposed to the problems of racial minorities in such a way that they become more supportive of the concerns of minority group members.

ADVANTAGES OF MULTIRACIAL CHURCHES

The concerns of the church growth specialists and the cultural pluralists are legitimate. I have provided answers for at least some of their concerns. Yet if there are not advantages to having multiracial churches in the United States, then it is reasonable to ask why we should undertake the effort necessary to create and sustain them. I contend that there are advantages to having these churches that outweigh any potential problems. Here are some of them.

1. Reaching multiracial communities. I have previously suggested that contemporary Americans are more comfortable and desirous of multiracial environments than they have been in the past. This is especially true of those who live in integrated subcultures. Examples of these integrated subcultures include college students, the fine arts community, Generation Xers. This is not to discount the fact that there is still a good deal of racial segregation in our society and a need for ministries to reach out to those in segregated communities. But today there is more of an opportunity to reach communities that are multiracial than there has been in the past. To reach individuals in multiracial environments it is important to have churches with congregations of different races. Individuals, such as my wife, who are now exposed to multiracial social networks are going to be more comfortable in integrated churches than in racially segregated ones.

A related argument for multiracial churches flows from the fact that interracial families are increasing in our society.[15] Because of this growth, a variety of new social and political organizations have developed to meet the needs of these families.[16] It is vital that the Christian community also makes an effort to minister to interracial families. Multiracial churches are an important way Christians can serve multiracial families. Individuals in interracial marriages and the multiracial children from those marriages generally need to worship in an environment where the racial diversity of their family can be reflected. If multiracial churches are not readily available for such individuals then they may choose to not attend church at all. Thus, multiracial churches are important if we want to reach this small, yet growing segment of American society.

It is of interest that I found several of the pastors of multiracial churches to be interracially married. Having individuals in a multiracial marriage leading a church can be a signal to interracial families that they are welcomed. This signal will be even stronger if the church itself is multiracial. It is likely that these interracially married leaders have a vested interest in creating a multiracial church so that they will have an atmosphere comfortable for their own families. The tendency of interracially married leaders to create multiracial churches should tell us just how important such churches are in ministering to interracial families.

2. *Racial reconciliation.* A second important advantage of multiracial churches is that these churches may be important in the promotion of racial reconciliation. I conceptualize racial reconciliation as one of the major ways that Christians help alleviate racial alienation in the United States. There has been a good deal of work within the Christian community toward solving racial problems.[17] I have written some of this work and argue that multiracial churches serve both as a natural extension of racial reconciliation as well as a mechanism that can help produce racial reconciliation.[18] Looking at the work of Christians who have advocated racial reconciliation helps to illustrate this point.[19]

Advocates of racial reconciliation point out that it is important that Christians learn how to interact with each other. They contend that since Christ calls us to love each other, members of different races must make deliberate attempts to interact.[20] Scriptural evidence for this principle can be seen in the story of the Samaritan woman at the well (John 4:4-42). Second Kings 17:24-41 documents the fact that the

Samaritans are a mixed-race people. Because of this racial ambiguity and the religious conflict that emerged from it, hostility between Jews and Samaritans developed. Yet Jesus went out of his way to go into Samaria to minister to the woman. Jesus realized that intentional efforts to create interracial interactions were necessary to deal with the historical hatreds and mistrusts that developed between Jews and Samaritans.

Given such an example it becomes clear that Christians of different races should go out of their way to worship together. Because of the importance of race in the United States there is a natural tendency for Americans to stick with people of their own race. Despite some of the increasing racial diversity in our country and the fact that more Americans have been exposed to different racial groups than ever before, we still tend to live in segregated neighborhoods,[21] have segregated social networks[22] and attend schools with members of mostly our own race.[23] This segregation makes it harder for us to develop multiracial churches since we tend to look toward our neighbors, friends and classmates as prospective members for our churches.

Proponents of racial reconciliation reject the assertions of some cultural pluralists who contend that distance must be maintained between minority group members and whites since European Americans continue to exploit racial minorities and smother the culture of the minority group members. Having developed their models within a multiracial context, the advocates of Christian racial reconciliation value interracial primary relationships over cultural distinctiveness. Yet this desire for interaction is not a reaffirmation of a so-called colorblind philosophy or mere assimilation.[24] While recognizing that there has historically been a significant amount of racial oppression, supporters of racial reconciliation still believe that interaction between members of different races is necessary to allow for the eventual development of racial harmony. They argue that past historical oppression has generated contemporary racial alienation and that using this alienation to justify the maintenance of a separation of racial groups is counterproductive. Therefore, it is necessary for the different races to learn how to relate to each other, build trust and establish a new relationship of equality for a process of intrinsic empathy to occur.

Spencer Perkins and Chris Rice document an example of this process in their classic *More Than Equals*. In 1983 a series of gatherings called The Racial Reconciliation Meetings marked a turning point in the Voice of Calvary's ministry. They were "the stuff that church and denominational splits are made of. Hardly ever do black and white Christians discuss their true feelings about race."[25]

Perkins and Rice argued that these meetings were necessary because "relationships between blacks and whites in America have been so strained that the trust needed to begin and sustain a relationship does not always come easily."[26]

Rice, a white man, had previously begun to consider leaving the Voice of Calvary ministry because he felt that he was unwanted and that blacks did not want further white interference. Yet through these meetings he learned that

> the blacks hadn't rejected me.... When they said, "You need to be willing to step to the side," I had heard "Step back." When they said "mutual submission," I heard "black domination." When they mentioned the importance of black leadership, I'd heard "No room for white leadership."[27]

Because these meetings became a place of frank dialogue between whites and blacks, Perkins and Rice can use them to illustrate how interracial primary relationships can promote healing rather than further estrangement.

Because of the importance of interracial primary relationships, supporters of racial reconciliation argue that there must be an intentional effort to create these relationships.[28] For this to happen in the Christian church we have to look toward the development of multiracial churches. It is easy for Christians who attend segregated churches to avoid talking with each other about the tough issues of race and racism. Since the natural organization of American society discourages primary interracial relationships, Christians have to take extraordinary steps to create multiracial churches. This exceptional effort to create multiracial congregations will reflect the importance that we place upon interracial primary relationships. If proponents of racial reconciliation are correct, then multiracial churches are essential for the Christian community to achieve true racial reconciliation.

3. *Demonstrating racial unity as a witness.* Every Christian has a responsibility to be a "witness." We usually think about witnessing as telling others about Christ. Sometimes we think of witnessing as living a life that others will admire. In their admiration of our lives we can then tell them about the God that has given us the strength to live that life. But witnessing is more than an individualistic endeavor. Just as our personal lives can provide people with a witness of God's might, witnessing is also possible though what people observe in our Christian institutions.

Unfortunately, throughout much of our history the Christian church has been as much a part of the problem of racism as any other social institution. While we can point to some heroic deeds of certain Christians involved in the Underground Railroad, the abolition movement and the civil rights movement, Christians must also deal with the fact that the Bible has been used to justify slavery and the extermination of the native peoples. Even today many Christian organizations still do not attempt to provide solutions for the racial sickness that plagues the United States. Instead, the leaders of those organizations prefer to avoid racial issues or to latch on to secular solutions, as opposed to offering a Christian answer to the problem of racism. Yet if Americans can see Christian institutions as a solution to racial alienation, then the message of Christianity will have more relevance.

Racism is a social and spiritual sickness. It is the disease that separates us from each other. We sometimes see racism as a political problem that can only be solved through government intervention. While our government has an incredibly important role to play, it is powerless to deal with the spiritual pain of racism. The spiritual and moral dimension of racism makes it imperative that Christians become active in healing our nation of this illness. Part of the role that the church must play lies in intercession and looking for wisdom from Christ. However, we also have a role in modeling racial healing. We in the church should be exhibiting how members of different races can live together. Yet when non-Christians look at Christians they often see that our churches are more segregated than the rest of society. They see that we have white evangelicals who perceive many black Christians as sinners because they are Democrats and black Christians who perceive white Christians as fallen because they are Republicans. These are not the images that are going to bring an inspiring witness to non-Christians.

Most Americans understand that the racial problems of our country are severe. Despite the advancements of the civil rights movement, racial alienation persists in our nation. Racial misunderstanding and animosity is common and uncomfortable for all of us. Many individuals, both Christians and non-Christians, desperately want to find solutions to these racial problems. We can offer those solutions if we have churches that model how members of different races can learn to communicate and love each other. This model cannot be one of superficial relationships where members of different races merely tolerate each other. We can already see that in our schools and workplaces. In the church we should find people of different races who worship together and can illustrate love for each other in deep, meaningful relationships.

Given this context, multiracial churches can provide a powerful witness to the rest of the society. The more multiracial churches we have in the United States, the more chances that individuals will see models of racial healing. Multiracial churches have lessons to teach both Christians and non-Christians about how we can learn to overcome the centuries of racial damage done to our country. They can produce the type of racial harmony that is missing at some of the finest universities that continue to work hard to produce racial diversity. When we produce this level of racial understanding, then we will have a powerful witness that the skeptics of Christianity will not be able to easily dismiss. I end this point with a quote from one of the pastors[29] in the Lilly study about the value of his multiracial church:

> We're trying to reach a populace of the city that invalidates the message of Christ because of homogeneity. They don't think it can be true. What about the people in India, what about the people in China? Their wife may be Japanese, and they're Caucasian, ... and their whole experience of the church is one of rejection, almost elitism, in the way that they would describe it. You can't escape the fact that homogeneity feels like elitism, every direction that you go. There are a lot of people in this city that will not believe in a message that is spiritual if it doesn't express itself in a global, holistic way. That is what we are good for.

4. Obedience to God. A final reason that there should be multiracial churches is that they are in keeping with Scripture. I do not believe that God intends most of the churches in a multiracial society to be monoracial. It was not this way in the early church. The society that supported the early church did not have the same concept of biological race that we have today. There were very important distinctions between different people groups by culture and class. Yet in these churches individuals of different cultures and classes worshiped together.[30] This diversity reflected a level of acceptance to all people groups and showed the supreme position that loyalty to Christ had among the early Christians.

It can be argued that segregated churches generally reflect the culture of their racial group more than a Christian culture. Yet the Bible constantly teaches us that no human culture can be given greater weight than adherence to our faith in Christ. The story of the woman at the well illustrates this point (John 4:4-42). The woman wants to discuss with Jesus the importance of where to worship. This is a cultural issue, which Jesus does not see as important. He states that where one worships is not worth discussing. That is merely a cultural issue. He is more interested in the woman repenting of her sins and accepting his gift of salvation. Monoracial churches have a tendency to focus on where to worship, who to vote for, the organization of the worship service and other cultural factors that Jesus would not see as important. However, multiracial churches have a good opportunity to overcome some of this cultural baggage since no one racial culture will automatically be seen as the "right" culture.

The woman at the well can be seen as a story of personal salvation. It can be argued that this story does not indicate a preference for multiracial or multicultural churches but merely that God wants to see people of different races experience salvation. The New Testament clearly describes a church composed of people from many different nations and cultures (Matthew 28:19; 1 Corinthians 12:13; Galatians 3:28; Revelation 5:9). Yet individuals might still contend that segregated churches are the best way to accomplish this task with people of a given culture being free to reach out to others in that culture. The notion of a multicultural church, to such critics, is that there are different types of churches for many different racial/cultural groups, but these churches remain segregated from each other. Peter may have had such an attitude. Early in his ministry he made no great efforts to bring non-Jews into the body of Christ. In fact, he had no strong desire to see salvation among the Gentiles and did not want to interact with them. In Acts 11:2-3 Peter was criticized by circumcised believers for his social interaction with uncircumcised Gentiles. But in Acts 11:4-18 God reacted to Peter's own prior refusal to interact with Gentiles. God made sure that Peter would not be free to introduce his desire for segregation into the growing church; he gave Peter a vision of animals that he had been taught never to eat and commanded Peter to eat them. Peter, being a righteous Jew, refused to do so—allowing our Lord to admonish Peter for his narrow, culturally based perspective. Immediately Peter is given an opportunity to demonstrate his new lesson and to enter the house of Cornelius, a Gentile, who would then become a believer.

It is a good thing that Peter learned this lesson. Believers who had fled oppression because of the execution of Stephen were scattered, and some of them went to Antioch. There they begin to minister to the Greeks and to add them to the church. This ministry led to the development of a multicultural and, from the perspective of a twenty-first-century American, multiracial church in Antioch (Acts 11:19-21). The church in Antioch was vitally important since this congregation was responsible for launching Christianity into non-Jewish areas. It is not unreasonable to argue that this worldwide mission emphasis was made easier by the existence of a multicultural church that could easily accept people from different nationalities and ethnicities. It is common for American churches to make a tremendous effort to support foreign mission work in order to reach people of different races in other countries and yet to do little, if anything, about reaching people of different races in their own cities. The lesson of Acts[11] is that ministering to people of different races in other lands is not a higher priority than serving those close to us. The church at Antioch teaches us that it is important to deal with ethnic and racial segregation within our own Christian congregations if we want to be ready to reach the lost in other lands. It is at least as scripturally important to do the former as it is to do the latter.

Despite biblical support for the importance of a multiracial church I am not arguing that a monoracial church is a sin, in and of itself. Some churches do not have an opportunity to create racial diversity among the members of their congregation because there is not racial diversity in the community around the church. Other churches may have a calling or mission that precludes it from becoming multiracial.[31] However, while not every church should strive to be multiracial, clearly in multiracial America more than 8 percent of the Christian churches should be racially integrated by the relatively weak 80 percent standard I am using. It is reasonable to argue that the degree of racial segregation in our society is sinful.

4

TYPES OF MULTIRACIAL CHURCHES

It is important to acknowledge that not all multiracial churches are alike. Some multiracial churches almost seem to happen by accident, while others are deliberate in their intentions of becoming racially integrated. Some multiracial churches are very evangelistic, while others focus on important social justice issues rather than personal evangelism. Some multiracial churches have a large number of whites, while the majority of members in other multiracial churches are racial minorities. Naturally these differences shape the various ways that being multiracial influences the life of a congregation. Before a congregation decides to become racially integrated, the leaders of that church should decide what type of multiracial church is desired.

The Lilly research indicates that there are four distinct types of multiracial churches. These types were found through a question on the mail questionnaire about why a church became multiracial (see appendix A). The question allowed me to observe the way churches originally develop their multiracial nature.[1] What is interesting about discovering contrasting types of churches in this manner is that I found consistent differences between multiracial churches that are associated with their distinct multiracial origins. This suggests that how a multiracial church is created has important implications about the type of church that will eventually emerge.

Those who start multiracial churches should think about the sort of churches they want to have since how they originate a multiracial congregation, or convert a monoracial congregation into a multiracial church, has implications for the sort of church that eventually develops. So, before examining principles for the development and maintenance of multiracial churches, I want to explore different types of churches so that church leaders are able to better assess how they can create their multiracial ministry.

LEADERSHIP MULTIRACIAL CHURCHES

The first type of multiracial church is what I term Leadership multiracial churches. Leadership multiracial churches are those that are the result of the leadership skills of members within the congregation. This leadership may come from the clergy, the laity or both. It may be a pastor who develops a vision for a multiracial ministry, or a group of deacons or elders may approach the pastor and influence that pastor to work toward the creation of a multiracial ministry. I ran across one instance where the lay leadership of a church basically fired their pastor because he wanted to move the church toward a predominantly white suburb instead of reaching out to their multiracial neighborhood. While generally the support of a pastor is critical in a Leadership multiracial church, a strong lay leadership can also facilitate the development of a multiracial church.

Church members in Leadership multiracial churches tend to perceive the multiracial nature of the church as being ordained by God. Of course, as Christians we believe that our successes are only possible because of God, but some Christians develop an even stronger belief that God is behind every move. They tend to adhere to a more supernaturalist theology than other Christians, and their ministries are likely to teach about God's ability to do modern miracles and healings. Churches that have a strong belief that God is behind every occurrence are likely to perceive their pastor as a direct gift of God to the church. This belief can strengthen the ability of a church leader to influence the believers in the church since the words of that pastor may be treated as if they are God's words. Such leaders are in a better position than leaders in churches without a supernaturalist orientation to persuade the members of that church that a multiracial environment is desirable.

I point out the tendency of Leadership multiracial churches to have a supernaturalist theology not to criticize these teachings but to suggest that church leaders who adhere to a more supernaturalist-based theology may want to consider using their leadership skills for producing multiracial churches. The members of such churches can be very willing to follow the direction of such leaders and make the changes necessary to become a multiracial church. However, it would be a mistake to perceive the laity of Leadership multiracial churches as merely following their leaders. Those who are part of Leadership multiracial churches also attach a certain amount of importance to the efforts of the congregation members in creating their multiracial ministry. In this sense, creating and maintaining the multiracial church is often perceived as a team effort and not the result of one person's dream. Because Leadership multiracial churches tend to envision their movement toward a multiracial church as directly ordained by God, it is perhaps easier for both the clergy and lay leadership of the congregation, as well as the members of the congregation, to accept the transition from a monoracial church to a multiracial congregation.

A couple of other characteristics of Leadership multiracial churches are worth noting. I found that these churches are more likely to practice the charismatic "gifts of the spirit" than other churches. These gifts include speaking in tongues and being "slain in the spirit." Furthermore, these multiracial churches tended to utilize a variety of different styles of choir and congregational music than other multiracial churches. Given these tendencies, and the high level of acceptance of supernaturalism within such churches, I assert that heavily charismatic churches are the ones that wind up being Leadership multiracial churches.[2] I do not know why charismatic churches are more likely to be Leadership multiracial churches, other than the fact that in charismatic churches it may be the case that the church leader's vision is typically the way all major institutional changes occur, not just a transformation from monoracial to multiracial status.

An example of a Leadership multiracial church can be seen in a large multiracial megachurch I found in our study. This church started out as a predominantly white church. Over time a few black families began to visit the church. However, the pastor of the church noticed that those African Americans did not stay. Eager to attract more blacks, the pastor decided to change the way he preached and the worship style of the church. In my interview with a leader of that church I found that the preaching became more charismatic in nature. The leader also described the worship service as being more "Pentecostal" than before. Furthermore, the head pastor decided to get the church more active in the community surrounding the church—particularly the communities of color. Because he was so well respected for his preaching abilities and pastoral leadership, he was able to effect major changes in the organization of the church with relatively little resistance from the church members. As a result of these changes, families of color began to stay and became active in church leadership. The church became highly multiracial. In this way the powerful ability of the pastor of the church to alter the atmosphere of the church was the major factor in creating a multiracial congregation.

Obviously it is not always the case that a church will become more charismatic to attract members of other races. There were occurrences of a church becoming multiracial after the charismatic nature of its worship had already been established. In either case, it was the power of the leaders of these churches to change the atmosphere of the church sufficiently to allow the church to become multiracial. Finally, while the abovementioned church is an example of how charismatic practices can help the leaders of the church provide a multiracial vision for the attendees of that church, it is a mistake to limit our understanding of Leadership multiracial churches to only Pentecostal churches. Other types of churches may also find themselves becoming multiracial because of the leadership of their congregation.

EVANGELISM MULTIRACIAL CHURCHES

Evangelism multiracial churches have become integrated because of winning members of other races to Christ. These churches generally have evangelistic outreach programs to help reach members of different races. Such churches may or may not target racial minority members, but such targeting does not appear to be important. It is the emphasis that church members place upon evangelism that produces a multiracial environment. Like a fisherman who casts a wide net that collects a large diversity of fish, if the fisherman is not discriminating about which fish are worth keeping, then there will be a great variety of fish in the net.

The research in the Lilly study reveals other important information about Evangelism multiracial churches. Evangelism multiracial churches are much more likely to be Protestant than Catholic. Furthermore, these churches tend to be politically and theologically conservative and are less philosophically ecumenical than other multiracial churches. Finally, Evangelism multiracial churches are more likely than other multiracial churches to attract members of different economic classes. These characteristics indicate that Evangelism multiracial churches tend to be noncharismatic conservative congregations. Some of these churches may be fundamentalist. This is supported by the fact that Evangelism multiracial churches are more likely to oppose homosexuality than other types of multiracial churches.[3]

This does not mean that evangelism is the only way fundamentalist or very conservative Protestant churches can become multiracial or that nonfundamentalist churches are unable to use evangelistic programs in their effort to become multiracial. However, the evidence from this research does suggest that the leaders of fundamentalist churches are in the best position to use evangelistic and outreach type of programs to initiate a metamorphosis into a multiracial church. Those who work with or for a very theologically conservative church may want to consider such programs if a multiracial congregation is desired.

One example of an Evangelism multiracial church was a fundamentalist predominantly white congregation found in the Lilly study. The church had enough African Americans that whites did not make up more than 80 percent of the worshipers—making this church more multiracial than over 90 percent of the other churches in the United States. How did this conservative church attract these blacks?

A couple of decades ago the members of the church started a bus ministry. This bus ministry was originally designed to gather up kids across the entire city. The whites in the more affluent sections of town were not interested in sending their children to this church. Yet many of the African American kids were starved for the attention the church members gave them. While the members of the church continued to send some of the buses into the white areas of town, the bus ministry began to concentrate on the black areas of town. At the time of the study, that bus ministry brought in about two thousand black children every Sunday. Most black children who visited that church did not join the church as adults. Some dropped out of Christianity completely, and others joined a predominantly black church as they got older. However, some of the African Americans did eventually join the church. Enough of them joined so that today this church can be classified as a multiracial church. It was the outreach, evangelistic program of the bus ministry that created the process that lead this fundamentalist church into becoming multiracial.

DEMOGRAPHIC MULTIRACIAL CHURCHES

Demographic multiracial churches are multiracial because of demographic changes that have happened in the neighborhood surrounding the church. These changes appear to be based on the surrounding neighborhood undergoing a racial transition. There are two social forces that work to create a more multiracial atmosphere: the adding of different racial groups as they move into the neighborhood around the church and the subtraction of certain races as they leave the church. In fact, many of these churches are undergoing a racial transition similar to that of the residential area where they reside.

Today the success of certain "megachurches" illustrates that people are often willing to drive long distances to go to church. However, there is still a significant group of people who prefer neighborhood churches. This preference is especially strong among Roman Catholics, as they tend to attend churches within their own parish or neighborhood. As the racial makeup of a neighborhood alters, the racial makeup of the Catholic church that serves that neighborhood is also changed. The data gathered in the Lilly study clearly showed that Catholic churches tend to become multiracial because of a changing racial neighborhood.[4]

Yet it is not just the Catholic churches that become multiracial because of demographic changes, as the data suggest that some Protestant churches become multiracial because of changing neighborhood demographics. The Protestant churches that tend to racially diversify because of demographic changes are more likely than other Protestant churches to be theologically and politically liberal. They are also more ecumenical than other multiracial churches.[5] These facts indicate that Protestant Demographic multiracial churches are more likely to be mainline in their religious orientation.

One of the results of creating a multiracial church through demographic changes is that the members of the churches often do not develop close ties with other church members. The Lilly research indicates that members of Demographic multiracial churches were less likely to develop close friendships with other members of their church in general, and with members of other races within their church specifically. This tendency may be connected to the overall nature of Catholic or mainline churches, or it may have developed from the fact that Demographic multiracial churches were formed through demographic changes instead of through interpersonal relationships. After all, if a church is being formed as one racial group moves in and another one moves out, then it can be expected that there will be limits to the ability of the members of different racial groups in that church to develop close friendships with each other. If one of the values of multiracial churches is that these churches allow individuals of other races to learn about each other through close relationships, then Demographic multiracial churches do not appear to serve this purpose.

The Lilly research suggests that Catholics and mainline Protestant churches that become multiracial tend to do so because of demographic changes in the neighborhood. This research also suggests that churches formed through such a process are less likely to create intimate interracial fellowship. However, this research did find multiracial Catholic and mainline churches for which the creation of their multiracial nature was not limited to demographic change. If a multiracial environment that produces interracial fellowship is the goal of the leader of a Catholic or mainline church, they may want to consider a process to develop a multiracial congregation that does not rely totally on the demographic changes in surrounding neighborhood. However, if interracial fellowship is not important, then this research suggests that the most common way for Catholic and mainline Protestant churches to become multiracial is through demographic changes.

An example of a Demographic multiracial church was a mainline Protestant church discovered in a neighborhood that was undergoing a process of white flight. A predominantly white Jewish neighborhood began to transform into a neighborhood where the majority of the residents were not white. As the Jews and other whites left the neighborhood, one of the racial groups that moved in was West Africans—who had a strong Christian tradition. Because the church did not flee to the suburbs, the

West Africans found the congregation a welcoming place. To its credit, the church began to make adaptations in its worship service to meet some of the cultural needs of the West Africans. These adaptations indicate that even a church that becomes multiracial because of demographic changes must remain organizationally flexible enough to make the necessary institutional changes to enable them to minister to the new racial/cultural group.

NETWORK MULTIRACIAL CHURCHES

Finally, Network multiracial churches developed due to the expansion of social networks within the church. Social networks are the family and friends that people have in their lives. Americans can develop social networks through the people they know from work, school, social clubs and neighborhoods, as well as their churches. Some of the members in our networks may be very close friends, while others are merely acquaintances. Through these networks, individuals may be introduced to a church and persuaded to visit and perhaps join that church.

In the United States we tend to develop social networks that contain individuals who are the same race as ourselves. However, many Americans, such as my wife, are much more likely to have a racially diverse social network. These multiracial networks can potentially develop through interracial marriages, multiracial friendships or integrated social settings. Individuals who develop multiracial social networks can have friends of a different race available to invite to church. Network multiracial churches develop because the multiracial network of church members diversify and there are more individuals from a variety of races who can be brought into the churches. There may be an effort at evangelism that can lead to individuals joining these multiracial churches, but that effort does not seem to be necessary for those churches to maintain their multiracial makeup.

Of the four different types of multiracial churches, the Network multiracial churches are the most likely to grow.[6] I am not sure whether this growth is because churches—whether multiracial or monoracial—that use social networks to recruit potential members are more likely to grow, or because it is easier to persuade people to visit or join a multiracial church if they already know someone at that church. It is possible that because of the fear that Americans have about joining a multiracial organization, or an organization where they are a racial minority, that having a friend or family members in that organization is vital for helping people gain the confidence to join. Regardless of the reason why Network multiracial churches have such a strong propensity to grow it is important to note that they do grow, and leaders who want to start a multiracial church may want to utilize this model.

Unlike the other types, Network multiracial churches do not come predominantly from any denominational or theological tradition. While Leadership multiracial churches are correlated with charismatics, Evangelism multiracial churches with evangelicals and Demographic multiracial churches with mainliners and Catholics, Network multiracial churches are not correlated with any of these religious traditions. Therefore, those who desire to implement a Network multiracial church should not hesitate to do so because of their denominational or theological tradition.

There are two other important ways that Network multiracial churches differ from other types of multiracial churches. Such churches are more likely to develop a multiracial institutional identity and to develop interracial friendships between the members of those churches. These differences may be important because a multiracial institutional identity and interracial friendships can provide an atmosphere where racial animosity can be lessened. A multiracial institutional identity means that a church cannot focus on the perspective of one racial culture and ignore the perspective of other racial groups. To do so would make that church a "white" church or an "Asian" church instead of a multiracial church. Interracial friendships indicate that individuals of different races can learn about each other in a more intimate manner. Such friendships can make it more difficult for racial stereotypes and animosity to develop. Network multiracial churches may provide a more harmonious racial atmosphere than other types of multiracial churches.

I remember a small charismatic church that is a good example of a Network multiracial church. This church became multiracial when a predominantly white church merged with a predominantly black church. The merger occurred out of necessity. The pastor of the predominantly white church had resigned and the number of church members had dwindled. Yet this church had a building. The predominantly black congregation was a church plant within the same denomination that did not have a building. The regional leaders in that denomination decided to merge the two churches. After the merger, the white and black members of the church began to develop strong friendships with each other. According to the pastor, they also began to reach out to their friends and family members. In fact, the pastor emphasized to the church members the importance of reaching out to friends and family members. It is worth noting that the pastor is interracially married as well. Interracial marriages also appear to be more important in the formation of Network multiracial churches than in the formation of other types of multiracial churches.[7] The interracial social networks of the pastor and church members began to create a multiracial atmosphere within this church. So, while clearly the merger of these two congregations was important, the social networks of the people in the church were also vital in creating this multiracial congregation.

It is important to note that these four different types of multiracial churches are not mutually exclusive. It is possible for a church to have elements of more than one of these types. For example, a church with a strong evangelistic emphasis may use "friendship evangelism" to reach out to a multiracial audience. Such a church may be an Evangelism multiracial church, a Network multiracial church or both of these types at the same time. The different types indicate general tendencies that have led a particular congregation to become multiracial or to start out as a multiracial congregation. While the majority of multiracial churches found through this research tended to strongly adopt one of these four tendencies more than the other three types, this does not mean that there were not also churches that possessed multiple reasons for becoming multiracial. Pastors who are seeking to develop a multiracial congregation should not make the mistake of believing that they must pattern themselves after only one of these four types of multiracial churches.

These four types of multiracial churches offer distinct paths that a church or religious organization may take to become multiracial or start out as multiracial. If the leadership of a given church wants to become multiracial as a goal in and of itself, then it probably does not matter which of these four paths are taken. However, there are other objectives that a congregation may desire beyond merely being multiracial. A congregation that is 50 percent European American and 50 percent Asian American is technically multiracial. But if the whites sit on the right side of the pews and the Asians on the left side of the pews, then the production of real racial reconciliation can be questioned. Unfortunately, during this research I ran into a church that is multiracial but contained a great deal of racial strife between the different racial group members within that church. This particular church was not unlike a school that had been desegregated, but this desegregation generated racial riots that would not have happened if the schools had remained segregated. Integration of our congregations, in and of itself, is not a panacea for the racial issues that Christians face. So understanding these different types of multiracial churches is important because ideally one should not be satisfied with merely having a multiracial church, but should also desire that multiracial churches provide some of the advantages outlined in the previous chapter.

Because of such concerns, I recommend that, if possible, a church use the paths outlined with Network multiracial churches. It is my opinion that these multiracial churches show the most promise for alleviating much of the racial hostility imbedded into our society. The Lilly research suggests that the members of these churches are more likely to develop interracial friendships and create the multiracial institutional identity that makes it harder for the ideas of racial superiority to develop. If a church cannot use social networks to become multiracial but still desires to be multiracial, then I would encourage that church to use one of the other three paths. Nevertheless, I think it is best if the path toward being multiracial contains some effort at developing multiracial social networks.

Because a congregation can become multiracial by using more than one of the four paths given above, and because of my belief in the superiority of using social networks for the development of multiracial churches, I suggest that most efforts toward multiracial ministry should contain an integrated social network element. For example, if a pastor of a predominantly white church notes that the community around the church is becoming racially diverse and thus more people of color are joining the church, then this pastor may soon have a Demographic multiracial church. Under such conditions the pastor may be tempted to make minor institutional adjustments to handle this new multiracial emphasis and remain an almost purely Demographic multiracial church. But my suggestion is to also add an integrated social network element to the ministry. The pastor should encourage attendees to develop friendships with individuals of other races and use those friendships to enhance the multiracial atmosphere of the church. Church events and programs can be designed to enable church members to develop relationships with members of different races—thereby integrating the social networks of the church members. The pastor can introduce an integrated social network element into the multiracial church and encourage the development of the interracial primary relationships that are important if we are going to see racial reconciliation within a multiracial Christian church.

Finally, I have generalized about the kind of churches that tend to become a certain type of multiracial church. For example, I suggest that charismatic churches tend to become multiracial through clergy or lay leadership. I do not intend to place a straitjacket upon how a church can become multiracial. A charismatic church that wants to become multiracial would do well to look toward pastoral/lay leadership to fuel this desire, but should not be constrained to only use pastoral or lay leadership. If the members of that church already have racially integrated social networks, then they should emphasize using these social networks to accomplish its multiracial goals. This chapter offers four proven paths toward becoming a multiracial congregation and suggests which types of churches are more likely to use these paths. But the values of the members of a given congregation, not blind adherence to a sociological theory, should determine which path to use.

5

SEVEN GENERAL PRINCIPLES FOR BUILDING MULTIRACIAL CHURCHES

When I was single I often wondered how I could impress members of the opposite sex. Women were quite mysterious creatures to me then. (Who am I kidding? They still are now!) I did not always know how to romantically approach females. Did they want a macho, aggressive type, or should I be quiet and sensitive? Were they looking for someone to take care of or for someone to take care of them? Should a guy impress females with his physical abilities or his intellectual wisdom? Over time I learned that the answer to all of these questions is "yes." Some females value aggression and want physical and outgoing males who will take care of them, while others like the quiet, shy, intellectual types that they can take care of. Of course, there are all types of combinations of these and other characteristics that help explain the different types of guys to which females are attracted.

Ultimately, there is no prototype male to which all females are attracted. It is a mistake for men to pursue a "one size fits all" mentality when attempting to understand women. As a Christian, I learned certain principles (i.e., having respect for those I dated and for myself; being content with who I am whether I have a girlfriend or not) that maximized my chances of finding the right woman. That has happened and I am happily married. But to get to that point in my life I had to learn to be myself, live out certain principles and eventually find the female who was attracted to who I was, not to who I could pretend to be. These principles can manifest themselves in different ways for various young men, but they are invaluable in helping those men develop healthy dating and eventually marital relationships.

Sometimes church ministries seek a "one size fits all" mentality when attempting a new task, such as developing or maintaining a multiracial congregation. Just as I sought to find the set of qualities that would automatically guarantee success with females, these churches seek a set of actions that guarantee success in their novel endeavors. They want to know that if they do A and then B that they will have a successful multiracial ministry. Such ministries may have to learn what I learned as a single man—that it is more important to be yourself and to incorporate important principles in ways that are consistent with who you are than to try to find a legalistic program that guarantees success.

Multiracial churches are not developed in a cookie-cutter factory. They differ in many ways. Yet my research indicates that successful multiracial ministries clearly share certain principles that contribute to their success. How they implement those principles vary with each church as they adapt their ministry for a given situation. I am not going to provide a perfect model that all churches can employ if they want to become multiracial. Each church must adjust to the unique challenges that they face. I am more interested in enunciating principles that multiracial ministries utilize to help them maintain their racially integrated congregation. The challenge for ministries that desire to become multiracial is to find ways to incorporate those principles into their own institutions.

In the rest of this chapter I will outline seven principles that are important to the formation and maintenance of multiracial churches. Each principle will be briefly defined here, and the following chapters will explore each of them more deeply.

1: INCLUSIVE WORSHIP

It is extremely important that the worship styles of multiracial churches are inclusive in nature. What I mean by an inclusive worship style is a worship style that includes the cultural elements of more than one racial group. Inclusive worship means that the congregation does not limit itself to a worship style that is identified with only one racial culture. How we worship can be an important way to symbolize acceptance. An inclusive worship style communicates to visitors of different races that they and their culture are respected. Therefore, it is vitally important to include worship style elements from the racial groups that a ministry hopes to reach.

2: DIVERSE LEADERSHIP

Most of the multiracial churches discovered in the Lilly study had racially diverse leadership. This leadership tended to reflect the racial diversity of the church members. If the official clergy leadership was not always racially diverse, then generally the lay leadership (elders, deacons) was racially integrated. This diversity was generally not an accident since these churches tended to be aware of the importance of diverse leadership. Multiracial leadership is important because members of different racial groups desire to feel represented by the members of the church, especially racial minorities who historically have received a lack of respect for their opinions and perspectives.

3: AN OVERARCHING GOAL

Surprisingly, very few of the churches in the study made being multiracial a primary focus of their church. Rather, multiracial churches tended to have a goal that was aided by the fact that the church was multiracial. I speculate that having a goal separate from racial issues is important for helping to "sell" the members of the church on the importance of becoming multiracial. There is a certain amount of racial fatigue in our society. People are tired of discussing racial issues and trying to solve racial problems. But if members of a church are committed to another and higher goal—such as winning people to Christ or serving the community—then it becomes easier for those members to accept the importance of creating a multiracial environment.

4: INTENTIONALITY

It takes work to create and sustain multiracial churches. Their development does not just happen accidentally. Even when it seemed that multiracial churches were formed by accident, the leaders in those churches had to find ways to include the numerical racial minorities. This effort is related to the principle of intentionality. This concept indicates that a successful multiracial ministry will intentionally work at becoming and maintaining its multiracial atmosphere. Intentionality is the attitude that one is not going to just allow a multiracial atmosphere to develop but is going to take deliberate steps to produce that atmosphere.

5: PERSONAL SKILLS

Personal skills are the abilities of a church leader to handle the interpersonal needs and conflicts that arise in that leader's ministry. Theoretically, personal skills are important no matter what the racial makeup of a church. However, the Lilly research suggests that certain personal skills may have a unique importance within multiracial churches, since pastors of multiracial churches have an extra burden in helping members of those churches adjust to the transition into a multiracial environment. Thus, a multiracial church can produce additional interpersonal problems that require superior personal skills. The personal skills that the Lilly data suggested are important are sensitivity to different needs, patience, the ability to empower others and the ability to relate to those of different races.

6: LOCATION

Except for extremely large metropolitan areas, multiracial churches seem to be grouped together in a similar area of a city. These churches tend to be located in areas where they had access to members of different races rather than in the middle of lower-class segregated minority neighborhoods or in suburbs mostly populated by whites. I found quite a few multiracial churches located in transitional areas of a city—areas where whites are moving

84

out of the neighborhood and racial minorities are moving in—or in stable multiracial areas of a city. There the church can build and maintain a multiracial membership by drawing upon the residents in the integrated neighborhood. This observation is interesting, considering the fact that many Americans are willing to drive a significant distance to attend a church they enjoy. However, by staying in a transitional or racially integrated area, a multiracial church may communicate acceptance to people of other races more than a church that leaves for the suburbs.

7: ADAPTABILITY

A multiracial church must be ready to adapt to the new racial groups and cultures the church will encounter. A monoracial church has only a single culture to adapt to. However, by definition, a multiracial church brings into it individuals from several different cultures. Learning how to blend these cultures together is an important part of adapting to the new social reality created by the formation of a multiracial church. To this end multiracial churches have to be prepared to adapt to many new issues that will come up as different racial cultures merge together. Furthermore, the church members who have been there longer should take steps to learn more about the racial cultures of the newer members coming into the church.

There you have it, a very brief description of the seven principles of multiracial churches. Of course, such a succinct explanation is of limited use to those who wish to more fully develop or maintain a multiracial ministry. The following chapters allow me to elaborate on each of these principles as well as provide useful examples of how different churches demonstrated them.

Before exploring what other churches did to incorporate these principles, remember what I learned as a single man: you have to be yourself. I will not discuss these churches as specific examples to be copied, and I caution against merely imitating what other churches have done to implement these principles. It is more useful for church leaders to find ways of executing these principles that are consistent with the character of their congregation. I can only clarify what these principles are. It is the task of church leaders to decide if and how they can execute these principles in keeping with the traditions, theology and customs of their congregation.

One final caveat. Not all the churches in the study implemented all of the principles connected to the development of multiracial churches. Sometimes a church implemented only one or two of these principles. But, generally, those churches executed those one or two principles so well that they still became multiracial or were able to maintain their racially integrated congregation. My experience with multiracial churches indicates that the more principles a church implements, the more racially diverse that church will become. Therefore, I recommend that churches seeking to become multiracial implement as many of the principles discussed as possible. Yet if a church cannot implement all of these principles, it becomes important for that church to work very hard on the principles that are implemented.

6

INCLUSIVE WORSHIP

I sat in church ready for the announcements to end and worship to begin. I am an African American who generally enjoys the more spontaneous and emotional worship I experienced in black churches when I was a child. But since becoming a Christian I have visited and joined a number of predominantly white churches that had a more deliberate style of worship. My wife and I were visiting this multiracial church for the first time at the invitation of the pastor's son. The worship started off with a black gospel song in the spirit of so many songs I heard and sang growing up. It captured much of the passion and spirit of African American Christianity. Expecting another such worship contribution, I was surprised that the very next song was a traditional hymn similar to the songs I had heard in predominantly white churches. Such songs are connected to a meaningful history of Christian meditation. The third song was done in a Tejano style complete with a chorus in Spanish that I humbly tried to sing. My poor attempt at Spanish reminded me of the plight of immigrants who must deal with a new language in our nation. By the time worship was over for this multiracial church, I had undergone a whirlwind of different American racial cultures.

In this chapter I will explore what "inclusive worship" is, the importance of this worship style for multiracial churches and some examples of how such a style has been implemented within multiracial churches.

THE IMPORTANCE OF INCLUSIVE WORSHIP

Churches where one racial culture is dominant are free to allow that single racial culture to dictate their style of worship. However, multiracial churches are not generally free to limit their worship in such ways. Churches that desire to become multiracial or to maintain a racially integrated congregation tend to look for ways to incorporate different racial cultures into their worship. For example, in one of the multiracial churches in our sample most of the leadership and congregation was Hispanic, yet the worship music was led by an African American. His presence brought in elements of a black gospel style that was combined with contemporary Christian praise and worship. This gave the church a multiracial style of worship. As a result of this worship style, the church had an atmosphere of acceptance toward non-Hispanics—despite the fact that all four of its paid clergy were Hispanic.

This describes an important asset of diverse worship—it lends itself to creating an attitude of racial acceptance. The African American element of the worship in this church helped assure non-Hispanics that the Hispanic leaders are open to being influenced by members of other races. Despite the absence of racially diverse leadership, about a quarter of the congregation was non-Hispanic, as this church was able to illustrate its openness through inclusive worship.

The pastors of multiracial churches understood the importance of worship that comes from different racial cultures. One Catholic clergy stated, "One of the things that I always remind our person who assigns people to a liturgical ministry is to keep in mind the ethnic balance, to try and model that as a part of what of we do." Even though worship in Catholic masses tends to come from a centralized organization, which creates a high degree of conformity, this pastor attempts to incorporate racial diversity into how the liturgy is conducted and to allow the cultural expression of different racial groups in worship. If a Catholic multiracial church—which arguably has less flexibility than non-Catholic churches—recognizes the importance of adjusting their worship service to accommodate different racial groups, then other churches that desire a multiracial congregation should plan on creating inclusive worship as well.

Of course changing how a church worships is a dicey issue. Such changes can and do lead to power struggles. Christian leaders who attempt such changes should recognize some of the potential pitfalls that may occur in the creation of a multiracial worship style. They should attempt to balance the distinct racial elements within the worship style in such a way so that none of the racial groups feels short-changed by the worship style. One pastor said he undertook this process by

> not doing a lot of heavy beat-like holiness songs that many of our white counterparts don't know. They are not used to that kind of beat or music. On the other hand, not singing a lot of ... eighteenth- or seventeenth-century hymns that maybe some of the younger blacks may not be all that interested or knowledgeable about; trying to do a little bit of everything at a different time.

The challenge for multiracial churches is to find a balance of different worship styles that will enable these churches to attract members of different racial groups. It also becomes important to incorporate inclusive worship leaders into multiracial churches so that they can develop a worship style that is welcoming to members of various racial cultures.

DIFFERENT WAYS TO FIND AN INCLUSIVE WORSHIP STYLE

If a church has not yet developed such an inclusive style of worship, how can it develop such a style?

During my research I visited churches that created an inclusive worship style by a variety of methods. Looking at how these churches created inclusive worship may be helpful for other churches that want to move away from a monoracial worship style. While it is important to look at these churches to observe ways this principle can be implemented, it is vital to not to attempt to copy exactly what has worked at another church. Each church must decide how it can best develop an inclusive style of worship within its own unique congregation.

One church resorted to writing their own unique songs and using creative types of worship like drama. These songs did not pay homage to any given racial culture, but were a new worship creation in their own right. The members of the church generally wrote the songs, enabling the church to develop a music style that could not be duplicated in other churches. In this way everyone who visited the church began at the same starting place, no matter what his or her racial background. There was no sense that members of one racial group were being given an advantage over members of other racial groups. In fact, this type of worship was so novel that it is likely that new visitors to the church found themselves intrigued by it. In an odd way, making everyone learn worship songs from scratch denoted an equality in social status for members of all races and led to an inclusive worship style. However, such a worship style is only possible if a church has enough members with musical talent.

Instead of making everybody start from square one, a congregation can develop an inclusive style by recognizing the songs of different racial cultures. The church I mentioned in the first part of this chapter developed an inclusive style of worship by including elements of several different racial cultures in each worship service. This type of worship service tends to honor the racial culture of several different groups within the span of fifteen to twenty minutes. It is not difficult to see how such an effort is inclusive in nature. The advantage of this technique is that most racial groups are represented at every church service. The disadvantage is that this representation may only be a single song and not enough to satisfy the members of a particular racial group. Network multiracial churches are most willing to use this technique, in part because the music leaders in these types of multiracial churches utilize a wider variety of worship music than other types of multiracial churches.

Finally, I want to point out a technique used by another large multiracial church. The worship leaders of this church rotated the racial nature of their worship style. Thus, the worship of this church would focus on one racial group one Sunday, perhaps use music with a Hispanic style, and then focus on another racial group the next Sunday—for example, worship that is more traditional and European. The pastor of the church argued that no one is going to be comfortable with the worship every Sunday since the style of music that a person enjoys will not be played every Sunday. However, he argued that when the church is playing a music style that a person does not enjoy, the discomfort allows that person to rejoice that someone else is getting to hear what he/she wants to hear that Sunday. When the church does play the music style that a person likes, then someone else can rejoice that he/she can enjoy the worship. In this way the pastor believes that members of different races learn to put aside their cultural differences and to make sacrifices for individuals of other races. A weakness of this approach is that a visitor who comes on a day when his or her culture is not represented may be turned off by the worship of that particular Sunday.

I am not endorsing any of these techniques over the others. But it is important to point out that these leaders of multiracial churches had to work at developing an inclusive worship style. It does not happen by accident, but rather it happens because leaders recognize the importance of inclusive worship. They work hard at incorporating inclusive worship, even at the expense of making their own church members uncomfortable. You can have a multiracial church without inclusive worship. But if so you had better execute other principles extremely well because inclusive worship is a vital tool for creating a tolerant racial environment.

THE COSTS OF NOT HAVING AN INCLUSIVE WORSHIP STYLE

Inclusive worship is so vital that sometimes, although not always, you can tell if a church is multiracial by the type of worship they have. The research team ran into a church that claimed to be multiracial. The clergy and the members of the church told us how proud they were of the racially integrated nature of the church. Furthermore, the church also had a reputation for being multiracial among other Christians in that city. However, when I attended the service I found that they had a distinctively African American gospel style. There were very few elements of any other racial culture. It was not surprising that less than 5 percent of the people at this service were nonblack.

Upon further investigation I found out that this church had been multiracial in the past. Somehow the members of the church watched their church become monoracial while still thinking they had a multiracial church. It is my belief that the African American worship style I experienced in that church reflected their racial reality much more accurately than the perceptions of the members of the church. This is not to state that this church was monoracial merely because of the strong African American style of worship. But I do suggest that the worship of the church reflected the African American culture of this church. Perhaps this worship style changed as the racial makeup of the church was altered or that change in worship style preceded the racial change. Either way, having a predominantly black worship style was not conducive to producing a multiracial congregation.

An inclusive worship style signals to the visitors and members of the church that it is not dominated by any one culture. When I visited the above-mentioned church, I did not perceive a church that was welcoming to nonblacks. This is in spite of the fact that the leaders of the church wanted the church to be multiracial and thus did not have overt hostility to nonblacks. But to the casual visitor, this church can seem unwelcoming to nonblacks since the music, preaching and program style of the church were clearly African American.

Imagine this church at a time in the past when it was still multiracial but when nonblacks were leaving the church. What if a visitor came to this church when it had a black pastor and about 70-80 percent of the congregation was African American? Given the dynamics that I have just laid out, there was a pastoral staff that wanted to encourage nonblacks to stay with the church, but it had not been successful. The racial makeup of the pastoral staff and the congregation created an African American culture that continued to unintentionally drive off the nonblacks. Nonblack visitors who attended the church could be intimidated by the high number of blacks in the congregation and on staff. Such visitors would need a signal that they were welcome and that if they became a part of the congregation that the black members of this church would recognize their culture. If the worship style of the church was based entirely upon African American culture, then visitors would not receive any such signal from the worship service. Despite the outer friendliness of the members of the church, it is less likely that many nonblacks would continue to visit the church. This is contrary to the result I noted in the Hispanic-led multiracial congregation discussed earlier.

Like that Hispanic-led congregation, leaders of multiracial churches tended to recognize the importance of inclusive worship as a way to communicate racial openness. They sensed that people who visit a church will not come back if they cannot find cultural elements to which they can relate. One pastor noted,

> If they [visitors] can find a place where they enjoy worshiping, ... if they can enjoy that experience when they come, I believe that they will be a part of it [the church]. Once a person has come in and they know that they are accepted, I believe

it opens the door for others to also be a part of it.

When a church limits its style of worship to only one racial culture it is sending out signals about who is supposed to be comfortable at its service. There is a subtle message that visitors to that church must either accept the racial cultural environment of that church or find another place of worship. I am sure that most of the time the leaders of the church do not intend to send such a signal. But for members of different races, it generally becomes clear that they are either expected to assimilate into the dominant racial culture of that church or leave.

An inclusive worship style is not a guarantee that a church can satisfy all of its members. If churches attempt to create an inclusive worship style in an effort to please everyone's cultural desires, then they have missed the lessons of this chapter. An attempt to develop an inclusive worship style is not important so that everyone can enjoy every aspect of the church's worship. An inclusive worship style cannot satisfy everybody since whatever style is used will make someone unhappy. But developing an inclusive style of worship is important because it signals a sensitivity and welcomeness to individuals of different races. It is important that pastors and church leaders attempting to create an inclusive worship style do not lose sight of the importance of this signal in a misguided attempt to please all the members of their congregation.

NONMUSICAL WORSHIP

I have discussed the use of music in my explanation of inclusive worship. It has been my experience that most Christians think about music when they think about worship, which makes the examples of the musical adjustments made by multiracial churches very useful. Indeed, the most common way that churches attempted to create a more inclusive worship style was to alter the music presented to the members of the congregation. Furthermore, the research in the Lilly study suggests that different styles of music were more predictive of whether a church had an inclusive worship style than other dimensions of worship.[1] But while music is a vital part of how congregations worship, I would be remiss if I left the impression that this is the only expression of worship. Christian theological explanations about worship tend to not limit themselves to descriptions about music, but rather to present a more expansive view of worship:

> Worship is the declaration by a creature of the greatness of his Creator. It is the glad affirmation by the forgiven sinner of the mercy of his Redeemer. It is the united testimony of an adoring

congregation to the perfection of their common Lord.[2]

Worship is our response to what God has done for us. We worship when by word and deed we acknowledge that we are not our own but belong to God who has come to us in Jesus Christ. Our worship therefore is the celebration of God's presence. It is a glad and joyous expression of a gratitude that springs from the very ground of our existence.[3]

Worship in its total essence is a response to truth. Whether we are standing and shouting praise or reverently bowing as we experience the presence of God, every proper response to who God is, is an act of worship. When we write a tithe check, visit the poor and imprisoned, or welcome a new neighbor with a hot apple pie, we are worshipping God. We are responding to who He is and what He commands us to do.[4]

From these three examples we can see that worship is not merely how you sing or what songs you choose to sing. These descriptions imply that Christian worship is a twenty-four-hour-a-day duty. A common mistake that Christians often make is to limit their idea of worship to only what they sing on Sunday. But since this chapter is dealing with corporate and not personal worship, it is also useful to look at a couple of definitions of Christian corporate worship:

> The outward visible or audible acts of worship which are done in public worship. It is composed of the forms, ceremonies, liturgies, order of service and various ingredients in the meeting which make up congregational worship.[5]

> Meaningful human action oriented toward the divine, celebrated communally and in public.[6]

These definitions make it clear that worship is not done merely through music. Worship also includes how the service is organized, the style of preaching used by the pastor or priest and the customs of the church. Understanding this more complete definition of worship is important since when a church begins to think about developing a more inclusive worship style, the leaders of that church need to begin to think about these elements as well.

I have attended a large number of services in both predominantly black and predominantly white churches. It is my experience that worship services in a traditionally black style are usually about twice as long as services from a traditionally white style. The preaching style is different as well. Predominantly black churches use a traditional preaching style known as the "call and response." Those who have attended a traditional black church understand this style, but it is a style almost completely absent in predominantly white churches. Finally, there are customs within predominantly black churches generally missing in predominantly white churches. For example, in most white churches a person can give both an offering and a "gift"—which is often designated for a special purpose—at the same time by stating such on an envelope. In many traditional black services there are different times to give offerings and gifts in the same worship service. The offering plate is passed around or the members of the church come to the offering plate more than once to facilitate this process.

In the church I mentioned above that perceived itself as multiracial but was in fact a predominantly black church, I found the service to be longer than a white service, the pastor used a black style of preaching, and it followed customs in keeping with an African American tradition. On the other hand, when I visited multiracial churches that were headed by African American pastors, I found that they tended to have shorter services, a less black style of preaching and relatively few customs in keeping with purely African American traditions. These elements indicate a church that is trying to develop a worship style, apart from just the music that is played, that is inclusive rather than exclusive.

As an example of this general trend, we can look at the length of the church service. African Americans are generally more relaxed about when the church service may begin and end. On the other hand, predominately white churches generally plan their worship services so that those services end in a timely manner. This difference has lead to generally longer services for black churches than for predominately white churches. One would suspect that multiracial churches would respect these differing time orientations with services that are longer than predominately white churches but shorter than predominately black services. The data in the Lilly mail survey indicates that the average length of worship service for multiracial churches was about 83 minutes, which was longer than the average time for predominantly white congregations (70 minutes), but shorter than the average time for predominantly black congregations (105 minutes). Such a middle-ground time orientation for multiracial churches may be yet another way that multiracial churches find compromises between the distinct worship experiences of white and black Christians.

At least some of the leaders of multiracial churches recognize the importance of altering nonmusical worship to accommodate different racial groups, as attested by the following quotes from leaders of multiracial churches:

The African Americans provide a lot of energy, they remind us of the issues that we don't pay attention to. Anglos provide a lot of time, they provide structural organization.... Everybody brings different elements into worship.

If God starts to bring people of color into your church then you've got to be ready to embrace [them], and then I think there are some of the changes that we talked about—celebrate certain backgrounds, certain history, doing some education, working on your kids. It's building bridges, and you can do that in your preaching style, you do that in your communication, ... and then see what the Lord does.

Interior décor can also be a part of the worship of a congregation. In a multiracial Catholic church that I visited I noticed a picture of the Lady of Guadalupe. There was also an icon that the priest told me had significance for the Vietnamese who attended the church. Not surprisingly, this church had large Hispanic and Vietnamese populations. This Catholic church, while very traditional in its musical worship, was able to recognize the racial groups that are a part of its congregation by including certain symbols that are valuable to those groups. Through interior decoration this Catholic church illustrates nonmusical ways in which to create an atmosphere of multiracial worship.

Worship is not just music. Worship also includes the way a church decorates its sanctuary, the preaching style of the pastor and the organization of the program. We must be careful not to limit our perception about worship when thinking about how to create a more inclusive racial atmosphere.

CONCLUSION

It is through worship that religious organizations communicate which racial cultures are important to them. To develop a worship style that excludes all but one culture signals to Americans who are not of that race that they cannot have input into the life of that church. Of course there are important logistics that have to be worked out for the incorporation of inclusive worship. Some of these are questions about whether translation of foreign language songs should be provided, whether it is better to have Christ images of different races or to take down all human images of Christ, how much of the inclusive worship should be explained to the congregation, whether the congregation should invest in different hymnals for each racial culture or try to find a multicultural hymnal and so on. There is no single correct answer to these logistical questions. Each congregation will have to try to find the best answer for its own unique situation.

Undoubtedly part of the fear many church leaders have about implementing an inclusive worship style is the concern that such an attempt may be poorly done. They may feel stifled at the idea of trying to imitate elements of a different culture. I admit that few people appear sillier than whites attempting to imitate Ebonics. Accumulating knowledge about other cultures so that worship that honors those cultures will be authentically created can defeat these fears. Since it is imperative that multiracial churches find ways to incorporate an inclusive worship style, it is vitally important for church leaders to learn about the cultural styles of other cultures—particularly those racial cultures targeted in the outreach efforts of the church.[7]

Much of the advice in this chapter smacks of multi-culturalism and some Christians have a fear of that multiculturalism.[8] Such individuals fear that multiculturalism may lead to a type of cultural relativism. But church leaders who are attempting to maintain a multiracial atmosphere or to develop a multiracial congregation have to learn about other cultures and investigate ways to develop an inclusive worship style.[9] This learning process is also important for helping leaders of the church decide which elements of other cultures they can comfortably include in their worship service. This knowledge will help the church leaders understand the cultural elements of other racial groups and thus be able to discern which elements of different racial cultures to incorporate into the worship service. Church leaders should not feel compelled to incorporate elements of other cultures that they are morally uncomfortable with as long as they are still making a good faith effort to be as culturally inclusive as possible. In this way learning about other cultures can help alleviate fears that cultural relativism is a natural outcome of inclusive worship.

7

DIVERSE LEADERSHIP

I had interviewed a pastor from this church the previous year but did not get a chance to attend the worship service when I previously visited the city. But now I came back to this area for an academic conference and managed to slip into the worship service. The church, perhaps the largest multiracial church I had ever found, was huge, with many different races and nationalities coming together to worship the Lord. As the worship service began, a white woman came to the front to make a series of announcements. As she sat down, a man who looked Middle Eastern went to the pulpit. He was a clergy member with a special program coming up and wanted to talk about that program. After the choir sang, a Latino man came up and began to lead us in praise choruses. Finally, it was time for the preaching. The white male pastor stood up and began to teach. There had been a kaleidoscope of colors displayed from the pulpit area. From my interview the year before I knew that the youth pastor was black. Thus, white, black, Hispanic and Middle Eastern (or Asian) were clearly represented in the leadership of this church for all to see.

In a multiracial church people are often concerned that their racial group will be ignored when it comes to decision making. One of the most efficient ways to answer this concern is by diversifying the pulpit. If we find members of our own race represented in the leadership roles of that church then we can have a relatively high amount of confidence that members of that church are sensitive to the concerns of our racial culture, that they want to make it easier for people of our race to join the church, and that we can have a leadership role in the church if we are spiritually qualified.

Multiracial leadership increases the chance that the decision makers of the church will be sensitive to the perspectives of people of different races. This type of leadership models racial acceptance for the members of that church and creates an atmosphere of racial tolerance. While there are churches without multiracial leadership that are very accepting and supportive of members of different races, it is more difficult for these churches to express this acceptance and support because they lack multiracial leadership. For this reason it was not a surprise that most of the multiracial churches found in the Lilly study were racially integrated in both their clergy and lay leadership.[1] When the pastors of these churches were interviewed, we found that this multiracial leadership was not an accident.

THE IMPORTANCE OF MULTIRACIAL LEADERSHIP

Sometimes racially diverse leadership can happen quite naturally. But generally diverse leadership is deliberately created within multiracial churches. We live in a racially segregated society and usually have friends and contacts of our own race. This means that we tend to locate leaders who are of the same race as ourselves and have to make extra efforts to find leaders of different races. We may even have to resist hiring or appointing leaders of our own race. Thus, the effort multiracial churches make to obtain racially diverse leadership is an excellent predictor of whether that church will have leaders from different racial groups.

Racially diverse leadership helps facilitate the maintenance of multiracial congregations in several ways. First, racially diverse leadership was more common among Leadership multiracial churches than any of the other three types.[2] Since the leaders of such churches tend to have a great deal of power and authority, it seems likely that the racial diversity of the leadership helps them create an atmosphere of racial acceptance. Furthermore, it is to be likely difficult for even a charismatic church leader to convince the congregation to make changes that produce racial diversity if that head pastor/priest has not already diversified the clergy and staff.

Second, racially diverse leadership seems to be especially important for attracting African Americans into multiracial churches, as congregations with racially diverse leadership were more likely to attract blacks than other multiracial churches. The degree of alienation that African Americans face is usually greater than that of other racial groups,[3] and as such blacks need more assurances than other racial minorities that their concerns will be heard in the church. If this is true, then I suggest that any attempt to reach out to a group that is especially alienated in the community (e.g., first-generation immigrants, an economically deprived group) should include a member of that group within the leadership structure of the church.

Finally, racially diverse leadership seems to play a role in helping promote an inclusive worship style. Multiracial churches with racially diverse leadership tend to incorporate more different types of congregational worship music (black gospel, traditional hymns, contemporary praise music) than other multiracial churches.[4] This might occur because having individuals of different races on a leadership staff can bring different ideas about worship into the congregation.[5]

But an assessment of the importance of multiracial leadership is not limited to my own analysis. Many of the church leaders of multiracial churches also commented on the importance of finding leaders of different races. When I asked a white pastor of a multiracial church if there was anything he wished he did differently, he stated the following:

> Well, I probably would say that I wish I would've focused more on the importance of really raising up leaders, really making an effort to raise up leaders to encourage the other races—the Hispanics, the blacks—really focused on raising them up to become leaders and staying with the church and working with the church. We probably would have experienced more growth in the church if that had happened.

From his hindsight perspective he could see how having more multiracial leadership earlier in the life of this church would have helped this church minister to people of color. Congregations that are seeking to become multiracial would do well to seek racially diverse leadership very early in the process.

Three other pastors also commented on the importance of multiracial leadership:

If you walked into a church that was all black, no matter how many times they have told you we are so glad to have you here, if you never saw a single white person on stage, you may love the experience, but you're not going to go back. And you say it's a great church but it's just not for me.

We're always looking for the right kind of people. One of the things is that we just make sure that ... we are trying to match the right people in the right places. And you have to deal with the issue of color; you can't ignore it, you know.... We want to reach our community, and if people came to church and it was just all black leadership or all white leadership, at some point in time people are going to say, well, is there a place for me? I mean, what's up with this?

For us, I think it's come down to leadership.... When you walk in on Sunday you're going to see a lot of Asian heads because there are a lot of Asians here. But based on our first year when we were 99 percent Korean American to now, there are Chinese and Korean and Japanese. We have on our staff, a Japanese, a Hispanic, two Chinese and now the four pastors happen to all be Korean. Okay, so we want to change that. But all the ad-ministrative assistants, like my administrative assistant, are Chinese. The finance person's administrative assistant is Chinese. One of the pastoral interns who is now a full-time pastor, a female, is Japanese. So we actually have quite a mix.

The last example was a church that is currently multiethnic and not yet multiracial. However, the pastor of the church is currently attempting to make the church multiracial and has already succeeded in turning a church with only one predominantly Asian ethnicity into a multiethnic Asian church. People who understand Asian American culture know that the barriers between different Asian ethnic groups in the United States can be very wide. His explanation about the role of multiethnic leadership in helping his church become more ethnically diverse can also be applied to those who seek multiracial congregations.

EFFORTS AT CREATING MULTIRACIAL LEADERSHIP

To obtain racially diverse leadership, a congregation must be proactive and intentional in its efforts to find such leaders. It became clear through the interviews conducted with the pastors and leaders of multiracial churches that racially diverse leadership was not just a value for these individuals, but that they made efforts to achieve this leadership. A couple of the pastors commented on the efforts they undertook to obtain racially diverse leadership.

Q: If others—and I know people probably come to you with these kinds of questions—wanted to move into this sort of ministry, what recommendations would you give them, having experienced actually doing it?

My straightforward answer I usually give people is to hire a youth pastor that is the ethnicity that you want to move toward.... You just hire a youth pastor of whatever ethnicity is the next step that can be reached because youth tend to be more open than adults a lot of times.

I just hired from college a young black man who is a great guy.... That's a great hire for us in a lot of different ways. First of all, I've watched him minister for a year and I know what he can do, he is well qualified. Secondly, because he is black, it will say to the black people that you don't have to be red-headed to be on staff here. Our other high school pastor is a Hispanic guy, and we just hired the other staff guy; we hired another Hispanic guy as well. So we intentionalize.... In fact, I just turned down a guy who would've been a pretty good hire but didn't really add anything to us in the area of the race issue.

It was clear in both cases that the pastors have a vision about maintaining or augmenting the racial diversity of their congregations. In both churches the pastors used the racial identity of the candidates for the ministry position to help make a decision about who to hire. In neither case did the pastors hire the ministers based only on race, but race was a significant factor in determining who would be hired.

These examples suggest that a key to finding multiracial leadership is to overtly take into account the racial identity of prospective clergy to be hired. It may even mean that a church has to be willing to not hire a member of the numerical majority racial group within the church so that a person of another race can be hired. Finding people of other racial groups can be a problem. In the United States our social networks tend to be composed of people of our own race. To find people of different races we may be unable to engage the same hiring practices we used in the past. If we hire people because they are the friends or relatives of others in our social networks, then we merely perpetuate the same type of racial leadership structure that we have had in the past.

While I am not an expert in church planning, I know that there are ways that multiracial churches can racially diversify their staff. For example, a church can advertise at seminaries that tend to graduate members of different races but have theologies compatible with their church.[6] Alternatively, members of a search committee in a church can attend Christian conferences that draw members of different races. At those conferences these members can set up potential interviews where they can impart their vision of a multiracial church to prospective clergy and see if that vision attracts a candidate. Attending such conferences also helps the members of the church racially diversify their social networks—giving them a pipeline to other prospective clergy for future hires. Finally, the church can contact other churches in their area that are made up of different races and that share their theological orientation. The leaders of those churches may have recommendations about people who would make good clergy. In addition to gaining prospective clergy or staff, contacting these churches may help the multiracial church develop social ties with churches made up of different races, which can pay off in future opportunities to learn about people of other races.

Some Christians may be hesitant to make these types of decisions because it sounds like an affirmative action program. These Christians may prefer to operate upon a colorblind perspective whereby candidates for ministry positions are theoretically evaluated based upon their abilities as a church leader, and skin color is not a factor in evaluating them. Those with such preferences are likely to be especially wary about the idea of not hiring someone of the numerical majority race so that a member of another race can be hired. I understand and respect these beliefs, but such ideas must be challenged if a church wants to increase its chances for a racially diverse leadership. Given the history of racial abuse that we have in the United States, it is impractical to eliminate racial identity from consideration when attempting to hire for ministry positions in a multiracial church. Clearly it is vital to hire someone who is a good minister and who has a theology that is compatible with the church. Those are important qualifications for leadership in any church. But in the multiracial church the race of the candidate can also be an important asset that helps a church move closer toward a multiracial status.

If we begin to think about how the racial makeup of the leadership can help foster racial diversity within a multiracial church, then targeting certain racial groups for leadership can been seen as smart planning. For example, if you have a predominantly white church but want to reach an Asian American population, then hiring an Asian American pastor/priest is more efficient than another European American pastor/priest. Even if this person is not hired specifically to reach an Asian population, the new clergy member will give the church staff insight into the Asian population as well as serve as a visual role model for those Asian Americans who do visit the church. In this sense you can get more "bang for the buck" by hiring a diverse staff member than by merely hiring those of your own race.

It may not always be possible to add members of different races to the clergy or staff of a church. This is clearly true if we are discussing a small church that can only afford a single pastor. But there are other ways to put people of different races into leadership. One of the Lilly multiracial churches was so small that they could only afford a single black paid clergy. But they overcame this problem by intentionally constructing a seven-member board of elders that had three whites, three blacks and one Asian. This board racially reflected the rest of the church. When I asked the head pastor if this was an accident, he clearly enunciated that a diverse board of elders was desirable to help deal with the issues that develop in his multiracial church. The need for racially diverse leadership is not limited to paid clergy.

CULTURAL BARRIERS TO DIVERSE LEADERSHIP

There is a problem regarding the creation of racially diverse leadership that deserves special attention. This problem is the fact that we tend to have cultural barriers that prevent us from perceiving who might be a competent leader. This issue is deeply ingrained in the colorblind approach that some Christians believe is the best way to find church leaders. There are two major problems with a colorblind approach to leadership. First, as I have already discussed, our social networks tend to be racially segregated, so that unless we make special efforts to find people of different races, the "most qualified person" will often look just like us. Second, we are often blind to our own cultural biases. These biases lead us to believe that our own cultural norms are the best. We then put a spiritual value on a cultural value that has no spiritual importance. When we do not recognize the power of our cultural biases, we often fail to see how we justify the leadership potential of a prospective leader upon our own cultural bias instead of upon a scripturally based criteria. One of the pastors in the study illustrates this point perhaps better than I can.

> If you are Swedish or German, part of being a godly person is being early. So if you're on time or a few minutes late you have real character issues. But if you're a Latino, being on time is being early a lot of times and being a few minutes late is being on time, so what's the problem?! You have some developmental problem or you're over-fixated on time and punctuality and so you could eliminate all Latinos for leadership because of this character flaw.

This pastor goes on later:

> There are Latinos in this community, and Sunday night was a huge thing for them for family. So if you have someone come to Christ, know that [for] their whole family, ... Sunday is a big day for them. But here, if you are not in a small group on Sunday night you couldn't be in leadership. So

a person becomes a brand new Christian and they have to decide whether they are going to break off from their grandparents and great-grandparents and cousins and uncles on Sunday afternoon, a tradition they have been doing all their lives, or whether they are going to go to the small group that is demanded here for growth in leadership. If you are not in a small group you are not considered truly a follower of Christ, you are not considered really committed, and you can never move into leadership. At the same time it is supposed to be evangelistic—but they just violated their whole family because if they abandon that cultural time together, they have chosen the church over the whole family system. Little nuances like that become pretty significant, and you have to think this through if you are truly going to become a multiracial, multiethnic congregation.

The comments of this pastor reveal that often cultural differences that have nothing to do with Christian leadership can unintentionally disqualify people of other races from leadership positions. It is vital that leaders of potential or actual multiracial churches think through which characteristics are truly vital for leadership and which are culturally constructed. The elimination of culturally constructed criteria will greatly enhance the ability of a church to recruit leaders of different races. As we more fully appreciate the need for racially diverse leadership, it becomes clear that a church may have to redefine its notions of leadership to accommodate this need. When we can move beyond our own cultural constraints we can be open to what people in other cultures have to offer.

A common way we mistakenly use our cultural bias is in our evaluation of competency for Christian leadership. For example, communication styles tend to differ between whites and blacks. African Americans are more likely to have a more expressive communication style than European Americans. In other words, blacks sometimes tend to talk louder and be more emotive than whites. Their volume is not a sign of anger, as it tends to be among whites, but rather, among African Americans it denotes passion.

Let us pretend that a predominantly black congregation is looking for an education minister. Assume that this church wants to become more multiracial and thus would prefer to hire a white staff member. However, the whites interviewed do not tend to exhibit much passion toward the members of the search committee of this church. In other words, when they are interacting with committee members they do not communicate as loudly and emotionally as the African Americans in that church. If this church is not careful, they are likely to eliminate perfectly good candidates for the position because they perceive those candidates as being subdued, rather than recognizing that a cultural difference is creating this interpretation. Of course, the flip side to this analogy is that white churches may avoid hiring blacks because they are seen as too emotional and thus too unstable to be good Christian pastors.

Yet it can be these very cultural differences that these candidates offer that will help the leadership of that church be more equipped to reach out to members of other races. Multiracial churches must take care not to let such cultural differences eliminate good candidates from consideration. Learning how to tolerate and appreciate cultural differences in the leadership styles of people from other races is vital in the construction of a multiracial staff.

WHAT A RACIALLY DIVERSE LEADERSHIP IS NOT

Defining what I do not mean about racially diverse leadership will help the reader to focus more on what I do assert is important.

Racially diverse leadership is not the acceptance of a theology different from your own church. Accepting a different style of leadership is one thing. Accepting beliefs that are counter to the core beliefs of your church is something quite different. Within all racial groups there are those from fundamentalist, evangelical, mainline and liberal theological traditions. There is no need for a church to accept onto their staff an individual who does not agree with the way that this church basically interprets the Scriptures. In fact, it is my opinion that theological differences on a congregational staff are much more deadly to the cohesiveness of that staff than racial differences. Nothing in this chapter should be interpreted as an assertion that a church must accept individuals with incompatible theological beliefs in order to be multiracial.

Racially diverse leadership does not mean hiring individuals who are unqualified. A misconception about affirmative action is that it allows companies to hire racial minorities who are not qualified for the position. Actually, companies that can demonstrate that they have made a good faith effort to hire racial minorities but cannot find any who are qualified are operating within the parameters of affirmative action. What affirmative action does is force those companies to make that good faith effort. Likewise, nothing in this chapter should be construed to mean that churches should hire those without experience or training for their staff. Rather, I am calling churches to alter the way they look for leaders and to overtly acknowledge the value of diversifying their leadership staff. However, do not use the call for "qualified" leaders as an excuse to ignore the talented people of different races who may serve you well on your staffs and lay leadership boards. If necessary, pray for the patience needed to allow the search committees in your church to locate those qualified people of other races. For most churches, if they place a much higher value on finding church leaders of different races, then they will find qualified leaders to hire.

Racially diverse leadership is not a call for quotas. Just because half of a congregation is Vietnamese does not mean that half of the ministerial staff must be Vietnamese. It is true that such a church would do well to have some Vietnamese ministers on staff, but this chapter is not a call for direct proportionality. In fact, a multiracial church may want to hire members of racial groups that are not yet well represented in a congregation but are groups that the church seeks for membership. In this way a church may even overrepresent a certain numerical minority racial group on its leadership staff. However, attempts to exactly match the racial makeup of the congregation can seem artificial and stifling.

CONCLUSION

It is vital for multiracial churches to find both clergy and lay leaders of different races. It is important that churches intentionally look for people of different races to take up leadership roles. Such efforts may seem contrived and "politically correct," but they are important for illustrating to members of racial groups who are not in the numerical majority that they have a voice. These efforts are also important because multiracial leadership is likely to become the basis for implementing other principles of multiracial ministry. Often the foundation of many multiracial churches is the effort to create racially diverse leadership. I make this argument because these principles are not disconnected from each other. Racially diverse leadership will help potential multiracial congregations value and put into practice some of the other principles in the book. Designing an inclusive worship style (see chapter six) is likely easier if a church's leadership structure includes different races. It is also easier for a church to develop adaptability (see chapter twelve) regarding the cultural differences of nonmajority racial groups if there are individuals of that racial group in leadership. While all of these principles are important, the principle of racially diverse leadership is the principle most likely to serve as the foundation that makes it easier to implement the other principles.

8

AN OVERARCHING GOAL

It started out as a men's Bible study. Even before the advent of Promise Keepers the leaders of this Bible study had developed a concern about the lives of men. The head teacher of the study felt a particular call to disciple and train men, but wanted to reach more men than those within his predominantly white suburban church. He began to reach out to men with lower economic means and found that men of color, particularly those who were distressed and lived in the inner city, were more open to receiving his help than white men. As he brought these minority men to his church, however, he found strong resistance. To deal with this resistance, several families worked to build a ministry for downtrodden men in the middle of where the men lived—the multiracial inner city. Those people began to establish a new and racially integrated church, which largely consisted of the white suburban families, who were willing to take the time to minister and/or worship far from where they lived, and men of color, many of whom were formerly or currently homeless. Under the leadership of the former Bible study leader, now pastor of this church, these men learned to ob-

tain and hold jobs, forgo drugs and live a Christian life.

When the members of this church experienced some success with men, the church was ready to branch out with ministries to homeless women and children. If they are successful, then the entire complexion of the church will change as more women of color join this congregation. This congregation was not formed with the intent of establishing a multiracial church, since the overarching goal of this congregation was to minister to economically displaced men. But downtrodden African and Hispanic Americans received the message offered by the leaders of this congregation more easily than did European American men. And to reach economically deprived men, it was important that this congregation developed a multiracial ministry. The white members of the church learned to relate to men of color so that they could minister to them and had to change previous racially insensitive attitudes so that they could meet their goal of discipling these men. Their goal of ministering to men led to the formation of their multiracial ministry.

An overarching goal that is served by having a racially integrated congregation is another important principle for multiracial churches. As I studied multiracial churches I found that for the most part these churches did not approach becoming multiracial as the primary goal of their ministry. Rather, they tended to have other overarching goals that shaped the direction of their ministry. Becoming multiracial helped these churches meet their goals and was a byproduct of their efforts to fulfill the mission of their ministry.

WHY IS AN OVERARCHING GOAL IMPORTANT?

The relevance of many of the principles connected to multiracial churches is pretty easy to see. A multiracial leadership staff clearly models the racially integrated nature of the church. Diverse worship indicates a willingness to merge the worship styles of different racial groups. Intentionality, a concept I will discuss in the next chapter, is obviously important in helping a church overcome the natural tendency of Americans to stick with people of their own race. However, it is not immediately clear why an overarching goal is important for the creation of multiracial churches. Reflecting on why having an overarching goal can help a multiracial church maintain its racial diversity can help us envision why such goals are important.

Americans generally recognize the problems that racism has created in our society. However, most Americans are either tired of dealing with racism or are frustrated at the lack of results we have experienced in removing racism from our society.

Overt efforts to eradicate problems connected to racism and racial prejudice generally meets resistance from both whites and racial minorities. What may be called "race fatigue"[1] has plagued contemporary efforts to deal with racism. Efforts toward creating a multiracial church ministry can run into the problems of race fatigue. Many are not willing to put forth the effort it takes to create these ministries.

There has been a movement in the United States that emphasizes creating a multicultural nation. While many individuals accept this goal, other individuals reject multiculturalism. They are tired of extraordinary efforts to create racial diversity and believe that the best way to deal with racism is to ignore the social reality of race. Whether or not Christians agree with the ideas of such individuals, it is still important to be ready to deal with them, since people with such race fatigue will most likely make up a sizable amount of the resistance we face in maintaining a multiracial congregation. It will be these church members who will fight for the racial status quo and resist the changes that will be necessary to help convert a monoracial church into a multiracial church. Having an overarching goal is an important way to defuse the potential objections of individuals who resist changing cultural elements within a church.

If being multiracial helps fulfill a goal that is important to the members of a particular church or ministry, then it becomes easier for the leaders of that church to encourage fellow church members to put forth the efforts necessary to create a multiracial ministry. It is one thing to ask the attendees of a predominantly Asian church to accept a Hispanic associate clergy in the name of cultural diversity. It is quite another if the church perceives this Latino person as an important link for sharing the gospel with a growing Mexican immigrant population in the neighborhood surrounding the church. If this predominantly Asian church considers it important to give those immigrants a solid biblical witness, then the Asian members of that church are more likely to be willing to adjust to a Hispanic staff member.

As a proponent of Christian racial reconciliation, I wish that the desire to create intimate cross-racial relationships were enough of a motivation to produce multiracial congregations. But generally the desire to promote racial understanding is not sufficient for motivating Christians to work toward producing integrated congregations. Therefore, church leaders who want to create a multiracial ministry are wise not to put the main focus of their church on the effort to be a multiracial congregation. This is not to say that such leaders should disregard overt efforts to become multiracial. But efforts to become multiracial should be in the context of the larger goals of a church. A failure of a Christian leader to enunciate the overarching goals that are connected to the importance of having a racially integrated congregation makes it harder to obtain or maintain the multiracial nature of that church.[2]

PRACTICAL EXAMPLES OF THE WAY OVERARCHING GOALS SUPPORT MULTIRACIAL MINISTRY

A couple of illustrations of how the overarching goals of a church helped that congregation create a multiracial ministry are warranted. Notice in these examples how practical efforts to reach these goals led the members of the church to work at incorporating organizational elements that would make the church more appealing to people of other races.

One of the churches studied targeted the urban areas of its city for evangelism. This church engaged in different ministries intended to entice many of the twenty- to thirty-year-olds that hang out in the large metropolitan area. Furthermore, this church also desired to reach out in the arts and entertainment community in that city. Both the downtown urban areas and the arts/entertainment community of that city are highly racially integrated subcultures. Thus, the target group of this church was a noticeably multiracial audience.

To meet the goal of reaching these communities, this church developed evangelistic mechanisms that are not race-specific. For example, the church started renting a nightclub on Sunday nights so that it could have a ministry in the downtown area of the city. Since this area is very multiracial, the ministry attracted members of several different races. While developing an urban ministry was the goal of the church, the result of its efforts was that urbanites from several races were attracted to this "nightclub" ministry. In response to the development of this multiracial way of ministering to the young urbanites, this ministry began to enlist people of different races into the worship expression of this "nightclub." Furthermore, in an effort to reach out to the entertainment community, the church developed a worship style characterized more by the urban and art subcultures that they were trying to reach than by the culture of any single American racial culture, allowing members of a variety of races to feel included in the church. Thus, the goal of reaching the young art/entertainment subculture was a powerful factor in the development of a church with a multiracial audience.

In chapter four I discussed an Evangelism multiracial church that became racially integrated because of its bus ministry. This is another great example of how the overarching goal of a church can create the changes necessary to become multiracial. In this case, the overarching goal, according to the pastor of the church, was "soul winning." The members of this church take very seriously the importance of evange-lism. While many other churches also take seriously the task of evangelism, not many of them would undergo the expense and difficulty it took for this church to develop a bus ministry that maintains more than twenty-five buses.

Many of the white members of the church had little previous exposure to members of other races. Yet because of the importance these European Americans placed on evangelism, the members of this church were willing to implement a bus ministry that led to the multiracial nature of their congregation. The volunteers generally spent about three hours on the bus on Sunday picking up the black kids from their homes and then dropping them off. Because of the time the volunteers put into the ministry they usually missed the Sunday morning church service and attend-ed the night service. They also spent time on Saturday doing follow-up visitation on the children. Since there were generally four to five volunteers per bus, well over one hundred members of the church made these time commitments. This church, while large (Sunday morning service had about 1,500 people), was not a megachurch, and finding so many volunteers from a mostly white congregation[3] that previously had little exposure to people of color could not have been easy. Accounting for the time and expense involved in this ministry helps us appreciate the total costs of this busing ministry to this church.[4] These sacrifices illustrate just how important the members of this church saw the goal of reaching out to other individuals with the gospel. It was their drive to witness that created the dynamic that made this racially integrated church possible. This overarching goal provides the mechanisms that undergird the multiracial nature of the congregation.

FINDING AN OVERARCHING GOAL

If you want to develop or sustain a multiracial congregation, then it is important to use an overarching goal to accomplish this purpose. A vital question then arises: what should that overarching goal be? This goal must be one in which having a multiracial congregation aids a church in reaching that ministry goal. Obviously, a goal of reaching mostly white suburbanites is not a goal that aids a predominantly white church to become multiracial. You may be led to adopt such a goal for your church, but unless that church can also incorporate other goals into its mission, your congregation is likely to stay monoracial. The previous two examples from the last section indicate goals that encouraged, rather than discouraged, the inclusion of different racial groups because becoming multiracial was an asset in meeting those goals. In deciding on whether the overarching goal of a church can help that congregation become multiracial or maintain its multiracial makeup, a ministry must assess how racial integration within the congregation can help meet the overarching goal of that church.

Furthermore, the goal must be compatible with the basic mission of the church. A Protestant mainline church that does not normally emphasize evangelism cannot become evangelistic merely in an effort to create a multiracial congregation. If you are uncomfortable with political involvement then it is be unwise to develop an overarching goal of political empowerment of racial minorities. To make these types of radical changes would violate the nature of those congregations. To assess how to use an overarching goal to create a multiracial congregation, the leaders of a ministry must find goals that are compatible with the basic philosophy and theology of the church.

Given these two important aspects of overarching goals—a goal in which being multiracial is an asset and a goal that is compatible with a particular church's ideology—it is useful to speculate which goals may be most useful for certain types of churches. In the next few paragraphs I will attempt to match possible overarching goals to broad categories of Christian churches.

Conservative Protestant churches tend to emphasis the inerrancy of the Bible as well as the need to take the Scripture to people of all racial groups. Evangelism is likely to become an important overarching goal for multiracial conservative Protestant churches. As the United States becomes a more multiracial nation, Protestant churches may find that they need to adjust their ministries to accommodate members of several different races. As younger Americans grow up exposed to more members of different races, they are highly likely to have friends of various races. These younger individuals may find themselves less likely to stay at a church where their friends of other races are uncomfortable. If churches take seriously the call to evangelism, they may find that evangelism provides an overarching goal that spurs them into creating a multiracial ministry.

For many of the multiracial Catholic churches, it seems that their desire to serve their neighborhood leads them to develop a multiracial congregation. Those Catholic churches tend to see themselves as ministering to their immediate neighborhood, as compared to Protestant churches, which are more likely to draw worshipers from all over the city. It is relatively easy for black Protestants to drive from all over a city to a central location to create a black church or whites to create a white church or Hispanics to create a Hispanic church. But Catholics have a sense that if you move into a neighborhood you should go to mass at that neighborhood church. As neighborhoods become multiracial, it becomes important for Catholic churches to racially integrate. Because of Catholic churches' overarching goal of serving the neighborhood, these churches often find themselves developing multiracial congregations.

Finally, it is worth examining how mainline churches may develop overarching goals that can promote multiracial congregations. Such churches tend to emphasize dealing with structural sins and social justice. Many politically progressive white members of mainline churches have political and social goals similar to those of racial minorities. Yet efforts at producing Christian-based social justice are often segregated by racial groups. This may not be the most effective way to bring about social change. By creating segregated groups, white and minority Christians often fail to communicate with each other as they work towards social justice goals. If white Christians in mainline churches truly want to help communities of color, then it is vital that they work in close communication with Christians of color.[5] While this communication can be accomplished without having racial minorities in their congregation, having church members of color provides an important source of information for the predominantly white mainline congregations. Likewise, mainline minority churches can benefit from having European Americans in their congregations, as the majority group members can become powerful allies for them. Whites can provide important resources (e.g., monetary support, information) that will help them to work within the United States' social and political systems. This cross-racial unity can give mainline congregations legitimacy and insight.

I do not intend to suggest that connections with these overarching goals should be limited to the theological traditions discussed here. These goals represent different strengths of these three major Christian traditions (evangelism of evangelicals, the parish or neighborhood concept of Catholics, social justice of mainliners). But I do suggest that members of these traditions are smart to look within their own theological framework to find compatible goals for their multiracial congregation, even while it would also be valuable for them to incorporate the strengths of other Christian traditions.

OVERARCHING GOALS AND INTENTIONALITY

Sometimes a direct approach is not the best answer to a problem. A church leader can sometimes alienate church members through an overt multiracial empha- sis. If church leaders desire to minimize resistance from church attendees, it is valuable for a multiracial emphasis to be tied to nonracial overarching goals. Yet racially integrated ministries also need to be intentional in their efforts to become or maintain their multiracial nature. On the surface it may seem that this need for intentionality contradicts the emphasis in this chapter on the importance of nonracial overarching goals. However, linking a multiracial emphasis to other goals does not eliminate the need for church leaders to intentionally work toward creating a multiracial congregation. Some may argue that it is not possible to intentionally emphasize becoming multiracial and to having an overarching goal that is nonracial in nature, but not only are such actions compatible with each other, it is also critical that multiracial ministries understand and work to implement both principles. In the next chapter I will introduce the concept of intentionality.

How can a church or ministry maintain nonracial overarching goals and still make overt attempts at becoming multiracial? First, leaders of multiracial churches or those who want their church to transition into becoming a multiracial church must identify both what the overarching goals of their church are and how becoming multiracial fits into those goals. The previous section suggests possible overarching goals for different types of churches, but every church is unique and the leaders of each church must determine their own goals. Second, the leaders of the church must begin to convince the church members that becoming multiracial is important to accomplishing the overarching mission of the church. This persuasion should take place in the context of equipping the members of the church to fulfill the church's mission. This mission makes maintaining or obtaining a multiracial congregation vital to the members of the congregation for evangelism, community service or carrying out social ministries. Finally, the members of the congregation can then be convinced to intentionally work toward creating or maintaining their multiracial congregation. In this way such leaders can be intentional in their efforts to become multiracial even as they justify this movement toward multiraciality as an indirect effect of reaching other ministry goals. Thus, it is a mistake to believe that the principles of overarching goals and intentionality are mutually exclusive.

9

INTENTIONALITY

The church had reached that stage many pastors dream about when they get started. The congregation had grown too large for their old building. It was time to look for a bigger building. But the leadership of the church did something not typical of a growing church. Instead of looking to move toward the suburbs where many of the members of the church lived, they looked into the heart of the large city. More specifically, this predominantly white multiracial church looked at a neighborhood that bordered several different racial and ethnic minority groups. The white members of this church chose to leave their comfortable majority group environment so that they could minister to more economically depressed people of color. Therefore they intentionally looked to move the church to an area where they would be able to develop a more multiracial ministry. In that multiracial neighborhood, they found a Catholic church building for sale that had a school on its grounds. They purchased the church, began to have services and used the school facilities to serve children in the lower-class community. Close to many of the racial minority groups they wanted to reach, the church began to attract people of color in greater and greater numbers. Thus, the congregation became even more racially diversified as they moved further away from being a majority white congregation and soon became a congregation in which no racial group has a numerical majority.

There is a powerful tendency among Christians to believe that if they just welcome people of other races then such individuals will eventually join their churches and an integrated congregation can develop. But multiracial churches do not just spring up. They are the result of intentional efforts on the part of church leaders and members to create or maintain an integrated congregation. This effort represents another important principle in the construction and maintenance of multiracial congregations: such churches are the result of intentional work. This principle can be labeled intentionality.

Intentionality may sound like a contradiction to the principle of an overarching goal, but it is not.[1] The intentionality I am referring to works in conjunction with meeting that overarching goal—as pointed out in the last chapter. Leaders within the church begin to conceptualize a goal whose achievement is helped by being multiracial, and once such a goal is expressed to the rest of the congregation, then it becomes important to seek ways to reach out to members of different racial groups to help meet that goal.

If we begin to think about intentionality as the next step after a congregation has realized that becoming multiracial will help meet an overarching goal, then the principle of intentionality becomes very compatible with the principle of overarching goals.

For example, a church might have an overarching goal of evangelizing their multiracial community. This church can decide to meet the needs of people of different racial groups with unique programs that target the members of those groups. If a church wants to reach out to groups that struggle with English, then the leaders of that church may decide to use English as a Second Language classes to meet their needs. If the church does not put forth an intentional effort to help first-generation immigrants, then those immigrants are very unlikely to show up for worship.

Churches commonly decide that becoming multiracial fits into the direction of their church. To this end, unfortunately, the church leaders believe that if they make sure that people of other races are accepted if they visit the church, then a multiracial congregation will develop. This attitude appears in comments like those of the women in my wife's Bible study mentioned in the first chapter. But the social trends in our society are so powerfully geared toward the maintenance of racial segregation that it is unreasonable to expect the development and the maintenance of multiracial congregations if the leaders of those congregations do not take intentional steps to make racial integration a reality.

THE CONCEPT OF INTENTIONALITY

Raleigh Washington and Glen Kehrein first introduced me to the concept of intentionality. They argue that racial reconciliation will not occur unless Christians are willing to intentionally go out of their way to pursue relationships with people of other races.[2] Likewise, people in multiracial churches must go out of their way to pursue individuals who are not members of the numerical majority in their church. A laissez-faire attitude that waits for members of those racial groups to come into the churches is not likely to succeed.

The interviews of pastors of multiracial churches show us how they enunciated the principles of intentionality:[3]

> I think you can't take racial diversity for granted, that you have to find ways to promote and maintain that if you want it. Otherwise, because people are minorities by nature, they begin to feel left out. It [the desire to become multiracial] can't be a department. I mean, you can't just say, okay we're going to be multiethnic or give that to the missions

department. It really has to be right in the culture.

If I had to start all over again, I would be seeking out people who were willing to make a strong commitment to the church for a given period of time, interracially as well.

Leaders of multiracial churches attempted to incorporate the concept of intentionality. One pastor discussed how he began to develop his multiracial church in these words:

It definitely was the purpose of God. From the very beginning it was on my heart to have it. It was a desire in my heart that I believe he placed there and then he was able to grant the desire of my heart as well as all those who were open to that kind of thing. So first of all, I think it was just the will of God, the purpose and the mind of God to want to do this. Secondly, we're very, very neutral in many of our ministry programs. My preaching is not any particular ethnic style of preaching. We try to make sure our music is not ethnically centered in any one direction. Those are things that kind of came naturally for us to realize—that if we were going to be a church that was going to be multiracial and multicultural, then we had to be diverse or somewhat neutral so we made it easy for people of another culture to come in, to not have to contend with a lot of ethnic cultural stuff.

Clearly this pastor decided to form a multiracial church and because of this desire he took measures that would make this church more likely to develop. His attempt to be "neutral" indicated that he realized that special efforts had to be undertaken to attract people of different races. This pastor did not merely wait for people of different races to come to the church, but took proactive action to create a multiracial congregation. This type of proactive action typifies the concept of intentionality.

WHY IS INTENTIONALITY IMPORTANT?

In the United States there is a subtle norm of racial segregation. Even though Americans are experiencing more racial diversity than in the past, most children in our country still live in neighborhoods where the vast majority of people are of their own race, attend primary/secondary schools where the vast majority of students are people of their own race and have friends mostly of their own race.[4] When they are old enough to date and marry, they look toward people of their own race. Even though many workplaces and institutions of higher education are racially integrated, most of our intimate friends still tend to be of our own race.

Once we realize that we live in a racially segregated society, albeit one that is becoming more racially diverse, then we can see why intentionality is so important. If we go about doing things the "American" way, we will fail to develop many relationships with people of other races since the American way is a racially segregated way. Because of this inherent racial segregation, churches will naturally remain segregated unless the members of churches intentionally work to overcome the segregative norms in the United States.

The principle of intentionality conceptualizes the work necessary to overcome the inclination most of us have to stick to our own race. This work may involve efforts to develop an inclusive worship style, to diversify leadership racially, to locate in a multiracial area or to carry out other principles in this book. But intentionality is distinct from those other principles in that intentionality consists of the attitude that recognizes that achieving these other principles and developing a multiracial congregation will be the result of not accepting the normal way things are done in our society. This attitude enables us to be willing to go out of our way to become or maintain a multiracial congregation. It is probably not an accident that multiracial churches that incorporate the principle of intentionality are larger and are more likely to grow than other multiracial churches, since multiracial church growth is unlikely to happen by accident.[5]

INTENTIONALLY PREPARING THE CONGREGATION

It is vital to prepare a congregation for the changes that will occur when a church transitions from being monoracial to being multiracial. It is foolish to believe that major changes are not going to occur in this transition. The members of the church must think about those changes and be ready to make the adjustments and sacrifices necessary for the transition to occur. If the church attendees are not ready for this transition, then they will often fight against this metamorphosis, making the development of a multiracial congregation difficult—if not impossible.

A clear example of such resistance appeared in a church that failed to become multiracial because the people in the church were not prepared for racial diversity. This church was located in an area of the city that once was predominantly white and now was predominantly black. The congregation had hired an African American to help them reach out to the African Americans in the neighborhood. However, the white worshipers were not ready for this influx of African Americans. They did not want to adapt their worship service to meet the needs of the blacks coming to the church, nor did they feel inclined to welcome black attendees. The blacks that visited the church were soon uncomfortable and felt rejected by the whites. The African Americans left and did not come back. Their experience shows that to move toward a multiracial congregation, the members of the current congregation must undergo a certain degree of preparation so that the members of the new racial group will feel comfortable attending the church.

The dirty little secret in America is that we are a racially segregated society and we are comfortable with this segregation. Many people feel that to admit to this comfort is to admit to being comfortable with racism, and we do not want to be perceived as racist. Thus, individuals often supply a superficial level of support for developing a multiracial congregation, but are not fully prepared for the reality of racial integration. If a pastor attempts to start a multiracial church without adequately preparing the congregation for the transition necessary to become multiracial, then that pastor will run into the resistance that occurs when we ask people to leave their comfort zones. Multiracial churches will only happen when the people of the church can be helped to first recognize their inevitable discomfort, learn that this discomfort does not in itself constitute racism if they are willing to overcome it, and be adequately prepared for a multiracial environment.

How can a church prepare its members for the process of becoming multiracial? This preparation can come in sermons that lay out the values necessary for this task or in programs that allow members of the congregations to interact with individuals of other races. Often the members of the congregation need a vision to understand why becoming multiracial is important. The pastor of the church in the opening story informed me that he spent a great deal of time and a significant number of sermons imparting his multiracial vision to the congregation before undergoing the move to the central, multiracial part of the city. Here an overarching goal of the church can be of vital importance. If the leader(s) of the church can use the desire of the congregation to better minister to the community, to evangelize, to deal with social justice and so on, to help the members of that congregation perceive that becoming multiracial will help them achieve their goals, then the leader(s) will have gone a long way in preparing that congregation for making a transition to becoming multiracial.

Once a congregation has perceived the need to become multiracial, then the church members can be ready to take the intentional steps needed to make a multiracial church possible. When the members of a congregation take such steps they often make such a strong commitment to becoming multiracial that it becomes very difficult to return to being a monoracial church. After the church in this chapter's opening example prepared to become multiracial by moving into an interracial neighborhood, it would have been very difficult for that church to move back into the suburbs. The sacrifices the church members made in moving into the multiracial neighborhood psychologically prepared them for the further sacrifices that would be necessary to make the multiracial church plant a success, and those sacrifices would also make it too painful for them to move out of the multiracial neighborhood.

This intentional preparation is important for another reason as well. Even after a church becomes multiracial, there will be challenges and threats to the racially integrative nature of the church. For example, some of the members of the old racial group in the congregation may resist the changes that occur. Furthermore, members of the new racial groups may have a difficult time trusting the old racial group. To survive these and other challenges the members of the church are going to have to be willing to make the adjustments necessary to maintain the church's racial integration. The commitment that comes from intentionally working for a multiracial congregation is invaluable in helping a church handle the new adjustments that will come.

WHAT ABOUT WHEN DIFFERENT RACES JUST SHOW UP?

Sometimes multiracial churches are formed when people of different races just come to the church—seemingly out of nowhere. These people just happen to show up without any special efforts by the existing clergy or laity. I noted in chapter four that some multiracial congregations are Demographic multiracial churches, the result of demographic changes in the surrounding neighborhood of the church. There is a tendency to believe that these racially integrated churches resulted by accident and that the congregation was just fortunate enough to become multiracial without any effort. Sometimes the leaders of some multiracial congregations ex-pressed this perspective themselves. Yet I strongly disagree with this assessment. While the formation of such racially integrated churches may not be the result of intentional planning for a multiracial congre-gation, maintaining this multiracial mix is impossible without intentional efforts on the part of church leaders to maintain this mix. Even if people of other races just start to show up, a congregation still has to make efforts to maintain its racial integration.

For example, Catholic churches that become multira-cial tend to become racially mixed because of the demographic changes in their immediate neighbor-hood. But the multiracial Catholic churches in the

Lilly study did not take this racial mix for granted. Instead, these churches tended to alter the décor of their sanctuaries, alter their worship services or initiate social programs that would help them maintain their multiracial mixture. In one case, the effort of a Catholic church to alter its worship style to become more accommodating to different racial groups led to the church's ability to extend its reach toward other racial groups beyond its own community. When asked, "Do they [black members of the church] mostly come from the neighborhood or are they coming from all over too?" the priest in the church answered:

> Mostly here and then a lot of people are coming out of ... the southside of downtown, but it seems to me that with upward mobility they are moving up into the north side, into this area, the nicer area.... We have a number of families who are driving down from 20-25 miles away. This is the homestead parish.

The efforts that this formerly predominantly white parish made to attract African Americans were so successful that they were able to extend their reach beyond their immediate neighborhood. Merely because a church's multiracial character originated from external demographic changes that were out of the control of church leaders does not mean that a congregation is limited to these external forces to enhance its multiracial nature.

It is important that churches fortunate enough to become multiracial without much preparation or planning do not take this racial integration for granted. Churches that do not appreciate the social forces that create racial segregation in our society will soon find themselves losing members of the new racial group. But churches that build upon their original multiracial formation with an intentional effort to become even more racially integrated can find themselves developing a reputation for racial diversity and attract even more members from different races.

CONCLUSION

Becoming multiracial is generally the result of hard work by the leaders and laity of integrated congregations. In those few instances where a church is fortunate enough to develop a racially integrated congregation with little work, effort is still needed for that church to maintain its racial mix. Churches that do not prepare or work at maintaining their multiracial mix can, and most likely will, lose that mix. A color-blind philosophy that discounts the importance of race in our society does not generally lead to successful multiracial churches.

Intentional efforts that acknowledge the importance of explicitly dealing with the racial issues that will emerge in the construction and maintenance of integrated congregations are vital. The goal of this chapter is to highlight this intentional effort and point out to future leaders of multiracial churches that an attitude of intentionality will be absolutely essential. Therefore, I suggest that leaders of multiracial churches or those who are attempting to start multiracial churches begin to plan for the multiracial makeup of their church as soon as possible. Those of you who already have a racially integrated congregation would do well use the tools in appendix C to determine the type of multiracial church you currently have. In that appendix, I suggest ways you can assess what type of multiracial church you have, as well as ways you can discover which of the seven principles your church should strengthen. I recommend that you look over the items in table 3 in appendix A to help you develop ideas you can utilize in your congregation. The situation for each congregation is unique and I cannot presume to lay out specific suggestions that will apply to any given congregation. Nevertheless, the tools in the appendixes can help church leaders develop the specific ideas that may help them create or maintain a racially diverse membership.

10

PERSONAL SKILLS

It has happened many times. A predominantly white church was located in an area of the city where whites were leaving in droves. The church somehow had to reach out to the new minorities coming into the neighborhood, move out to the white suburbs or die out. A new pastor was hired for this church and began to work on the first option. He started out by making personal visits to many of the new neighbors of the church. His friendly and caring demeanor made it difficult for someone who visited the church to not come back. Many of the racial minorities were uncomfortable attending a church where the majority of the church members were white. Several majority group members were also uncomfortable with this influx of new racial groups. Thus, the church, although multiracial, consisted of people of different races who did not interact with each other. The pastor became sensitive to these potential problems. His ability to relate to people of different races enabled him to minister to both the white and nonwhite members of the church. He found another church member to help him empower the new racial minorities and get them ready for church leadership. He exhibited patience in helping members of different races find their place in this church. Because of the personal abilities God gave this pastor, this multiracial church has grown and thrived.

When asked about what they have learned about being in a multiracial ministry and what they wished they knew when starting their ministries, head pastors of multiracial churches consistently exhibited a desire to develop relational skills in an attempt to aid their efforts at multiracial ministry. The consistency of that desire among many of the pastors made it clear that such skills play a part in the success of multiracial churches. Identifying these personal skills and exploring their importance in creating and sustaining multiracial ministries is the focus of this chapter.

The development of pastoral personal skills is valuable regardless of the racial makeup of the church. In this light, discovering the importance of personal skills should not be a surprise. While there are obviously successful pastors who do not have excellent relational skills, having such skills will make it easier for a pastor to succeed. But the term "personal skills" is quite ambiguous. Many qualities fall under the rubric of relational or interpersonal skills. For Christian leaders to understand how personal skills may aid them in the maintenance of their multiracial ministries, this concept has to be defined. In the statements of the multiracial church pastors, I discovered which types of personal skills they determine most important for the development and maintenance of multiracial churches. The interviews with the pastors have allowed me to identify four areas of personal skills that pastors of multiracial churches perceive as important.

SENSITIVITY TO DIFFERENT NEEDS

The pastors in the Lilly study pointed to the ability to be sensitive to the different needs that people of various races bring to a church. There is an organizational component to this need that will be explored later. But right now I am pointing out an interpersonal dimension of sensitivity that has to be applied to the different needs of various racial groups.

This sensitivity has two dimensions. The first dimension involves the ability to receive, evaluate and appropriately handle criticism that may come because of the church's attempt to create a multiracial atmosphere. As I studied multiracial churches, it became clear that not all of the laity were supportive of the transition that churches undertook to become multiracial. It was not uncommon for churches to initially lose members when the number of individuals from different racial groups dramatically increased. Some of this loss is unavoidable. People who are uncomfortable with a multiracial atmosphere are going to leave no matter what the pastor does, even as many other individuals stay or join precisely because they enjoy the multiracial atmosphere of the church. However, there is a certain group of people who may stay or leave. These individuals may be uncomfortable with some of the changes that are occurring and with the presence of new racial groups, but they also want to help create a multiracial environment in their churches. A pastor who is sensitive to the concerns of such individuals, while not abandoning the goal of developing a multiracial church, stands the best chance of retaining them.

To retain these individuals, a pastor may have to endure a number of unfair criticisms from individuals who are uncomfortable with the emerging multiracial reality. A pastor who is not able to deal with such criticism in a mature way may not succeed in the attempt to create a multiracial church. As one Catholic leader of a multiracial church observed, a leader had to keep on "trying to be sensitive to where people are, developing a real thick skin." Without somewhat of a thick skin to endure the pressures that can develop in the attempt to form a multiracial ministry it will be difficult for church leaders to make the adjustments necessary to serve the current majority racial group in the church, as well as the new racial group.

The second dimension of this sensitivity that church leaders need to develop involves the ability to adjust to the various cultures and customs that new racial groups bring to an existing church. We have all had the experience of committing a social faux pas due to our cultural ignorance. Pastors who want to develop a multiracial ministry and do not have a lot of experience with individuals from different races should expect to make mistakes as well. The making of a mistake is not the end of a multiracial ministry. But it is important that a pastor learns from such mistakes and becomes better prepared for future interpersonal encounters with members of that racial group. A couple of examples given by multiracial clergy help illustrate this point:

> I have learned to be somewhat more sensitive with other people and to know that some things are very sentimental. I'll give you an example. The Irish have a saying, like if a kid was kicking the ground, you'd say it's the Irish in him. That's kind of gotten to where that's a compliment and I tried that on a [Hispanic] woman.... She got her feelings hurt. Well, I made a mental note not to say that again to people.

> Years ago I said something in a service that was very sensitive to one of my friends and he came in right away and confronted me and said, "I can't believe you meant this but I'm going to ask you anyway, did you mean to say this this way?" And I said, "I said those words, but what did I say wrong?" And he explained

it to me and I said, "Man, I never would have entertained that thought."

In both cases the clergy committed a social mistake that was offensive to a member of a different racial group. In both cases the church leaders were operating under social rules that were acceptable in their own culture, but their actions violated the norms and customs of the racial culture of the offended party. It is understandable if they thought that the member of the other racial group was being overly sensitive to the slight. Such an atmosphere can cause a church leader to become defensive about being corrected and to dismiss the concerns of the church member. But instead of becoming overly defensive, both leaders attempted to learn from their mistake so that they would not offend members of that racial group in the future. In this way these clergy became better equipped to operate in a racial culture different from their own.

In the two examples above, both individuals were white. I do not think this is an accident. Generally, European Americans are more ignorant about the cultures of racial minorities than vice versa. This tendency is due to the fact that most racial minorities know that they have to operate in the culture of European Americans to have a chance at success in our society, while such a need is less evident for whites. Therefore, white Christians who want to minister to people of color need a teachable attitude toward the culture of those racial minorities. This does not mean that such learning is not also important for racial minority church leaders, but given the dominance of whites in our society, minority clergy generally already know the importance of learning about European American culture and are equipped to be sensitive to the needs of whites that come to their church.

Finally, it is interesting to note that the Lilly data suggests that Asian Americans tend to be more attracted to multiracial churches that display sensitivity to the needs of people of other races.[1] The relative economic success of Asian Americans might make them less concerned about economic discrimination and more concerned about social rejection. Or this tendency may occur because Asian American culture in general prioritizes relational harmony and settings that emphasize sensitivity. Regardless of why this is the case, it does become clear that multiracial churches that want to attract Asian Americans should find ways to become more sensitive to their cultural and social needs.

PATIENCE

Another vital personal skill that came out in the interviews of the pastors was the importance of patience. It has taken more than four hundred years for Americans to develop the dysfunctional racial relations we have today. These pastors seemed to know that overcoming these unhealthy race relationships will not happen overnight. Attempting to create a multiracial ministry definitely has positive benefits. But multiracial ministry will also bring about unpleasant side effects that an impatient church leader will not deal with in a wise manner. Thus, leaders will need patience to be ready for these problems, whenever they arise. Or, as stated by a priest of a multiracial parish, "You have to assume the best in people but not be too crushed by underground prejudice that rears up unexpectedly." Even while this church leader attempted to encourage the parish to exhibit more racial tolerance, there was also a recognition that there will be failure and so patience is important.

Patience is not only required for abiding with individuals who show flashes of racism; it is also necessary for church leaders to succeed in sustaining their ministries. Most of the churches in the study eventually had to handle problems that arose because of the multiracial nature of the church. In some churches, there were struggles with white members who left the church as more of a minority cultural influence came into the ministry. In other churches, there were incidents of misunderstandings fueled, at least partially, by cultural or racial differences between the members. For example, in one multiracial church a white leader of the church had a run-in with a black salesman. This run-in turned into a racial incident, which offended some of the minority members of that church. A multiracial church may be a step closer to what heaven will look like, but these churches are still run by fallen, imperfect humans. Clergy who believe that there will not be problems beyond attracting members of different races into their churches are in for a rude awakening.

However, this patience is not merely endurance, a waiting for the problems to end. This patience should also be proactive in helping solve the problems. For example, these two clergy describe how they patiently deal with the problem of reaching out to the different groups in their church:

> Learn ... how to be more tolerant and just deal with people better. Be patient.

> Spend time with people.... It also takes time for the different groups to trust each other, to feel at home in this space.

In the first case the church leader was explaining the importance of troubleshooting the potential interpersonal problems that can arise as the different groups attempt to merge together. In the second case the pastor was discussing how to build trust between the distinct racial groups. In both cases the leaders allude to how they must incorporate patience within their personal lives to accomplish these important tasks. Both of these examples show that patience is a tool that can be used to empower the clergy to handle the new problems that a multiracial congregation can bring.

EMPOWERING OTHER INDIVIDUALS

One person, or even a single racial group of people, is not enough to deal with all of the issues that will arise within multiracial churches. One of the primary tasks of the leaders of the church is to help the laity grow and develop. This is true regardless of whether the church is multiracial or monoracial. However, the leader of a multiracial church has the additional task of preparing the members of the congregation for living within a multiracial culture.

It is vital that a church leader help facilitate a social atmosphere that supports racial diversity. The public speaking of the pastor or priest can obviously encourage this atmosphere. However, the social atmosphere of this culture cannot be established just by sermons and homilies; it also must be established by small group and interpersonal contacts that church leaders have with the congregation. Thus, a Catholic priest observed, "One thing I think is very important is to get to know people on an individual basis. That is very important."

However, the goal is not merely to have productive interpersonal interaction with the members of the church. Rather, there are important tasks to be accomplished through multiracial discipleship. To have a multiracial ministry it is important to teach individuals to become more accepting of different races, customs and peripheral values. One church leader described this process: "I believe in just really trusting people to be their best, assuming it, and ... then push people into their best inclusive nature." This individual exhibited patience but also attempted to encourage the members of the church toward a more "inclusive nature."

If a leader can empower the laity to handle the challenges of being in a multiracial congregation, then that leader will have powerful allies to help when times get tough. I constantly found members of multiracial churches who did not want to ever go back to a monoracial religious environment. This attitude came partially from the pleasures these people found in the racially integrative nature of their churches. But this tendency also derived from efforts of the leaders of those churches to empower them so that they would be powerful defenders of the multiracial nature of the church. The ability to empower other members of the church appears to be especially important for clergy in Network multiracial churches, as those church leaders were more likely to attempt to empower those who were not members of the numerical majority race than leaders in other types of multiracial churches.[2]

RELATING TO THOSE OF DIFFERENT RACES

A final personal skill that came out in the Lilly data was not much of a surprise. The church leader must also develop an ability to relate to members of other races. Clearly someone who is only comfortable operating within the culture of one racial group will not have a long, successful multiracial ministry. When I asked one pastor what he would like to learn more about so that he could improve his multiracial ministry, his reply was not surprising: "I need to be willing to sacrifice more. I feel like I would like to learn how to relate to people better."

The task of relating to individuals of different races is a difficult one. An individual who is unwilling to learn about the cultural norms of new racial cultures has a disadvantage when it comes to reaching or retaining members of that group. However, the leader of a multiracial church generally has a convenient source of knowledge for learning how to relate to individuals of different racial groups in the congregation: That resource consists of the members of the church itself. If the church leader is willing to talk with the members of the different racial groups who attend the church, then that leader can learn what might be offensive, what might be effective and what needs to be changed in order to serve members of that group. Such consultation was important for helping the clergy include voices of different races as they established the direction of the church. One Catholic minister put it this way:

> I think you really have to consult people, whether it's by way of a questionnaire or a parish council discussion or whatever. I can't assume that I know how to do this by myself.

In chapter six I discussed the importance of multiracial leadership. Of course it is vital to incorporate members of different races into the clergy, but this does not mean that laity of different races can be ignored. Valuable information can be gained from honest dialogue with those who live out their experience in the body of the church and who do not enjoy the esteem that comes with church leadership. Just as clergy should not ignore the average church member in the pew and only listen to the other leaders of the church in a monoracial church, a church leader in a multiracial church should take special care to hear the concerns of the laity of different races.

CONCLUSION

Personal skills are important assets for Christian leaders of all different types of churches. It is not my purpose in this chapter to suggest that those who lead monoracial churches can do so without developing powerful interpersonal skills. But these personal skills may be extremely important for leaders of multiracial churches. Clergy of multiracial congregations have the task of juggling different cultures in a way that those who lead monoracial congregations do not. While there is no one "right" way to handle this mixture of cultures, those who have the personal skills to handle this task will be able to create a healthy multiracial environment for their churches and thus increase their chances of promoting healthy multiracial church growth.

These are not the only important personal skills and this list is not at all exhaustive. These skills are only the ones that I have been able to document in this initial national study of multiracial churches. The four skills discussed in this chapter provide a useful starting point for helping potential leaders of multiracial churches think about which individual talents are valuable for those called to handle the distinct racial cultures in their congregations. A whole book could be devoted to exploring the types of interpersonal qualities that would aid individuals who take leadership roles in multiracial settings. But I suggest that leaders of multiracial churches start by improving the four personal skills learned in this chapter—sensitivity to different needs, patience, empowering other individuals, relating to those of different races—and then discover other ways they can use their interpersonal talents to support their multiracial ministry.

11

LOCATION

It started off as an Italian Catholic church. However, it was located in a city with a high percentage of African Americans and a high percentage of Catholics. It comes as no surprise that many black Catholics lived in this city. The location of the church made it easy for some of them to attend. In fact, given the propensity of Catholics to join the local neighborhood parish instead of roaming to find the church they like the most—as Protestants tend to do—there should have been a normal expectation that these African Americans would join this church. However, the racial barriers in our society can negate the tendency of Catholics to join their neighborhood churches. Thus, small black parishes in the neighborhood helped to maintain the unspoken Jim Crow norms that plagued this Southern community.

But three important factors enabled this parish to overcome the racist values of that community. First, the Italian congregation had the only church building with air conditioning, not a small consideration when summer hits this Southern city. Second, the Italian Catholics, particularity the progressive priest of the congregation, showed tremendous hospitality to the black Catholics who visited the church to escape the heat. Third, the church was located in a very convenient area for the African Americans. Thus, despite the cultural and social barriers against racial integration, this Italian congregation soon became multiracial. The congregation has remained integrated for over forty years and through four priests. The members of this congregation have learned how to over-come some of the racial barriers that crop up when people of different races develop intimate friendships with each other. Clearly, proximity alone does not account for the success of this parish, as there are many segregated churches in multiracial areas of cities, including this city. But the location of this congregation made it ac-cessible to blacks and aided the formation of an integrated church.

If a congregation desires to become multiracial, then the members of that congregation should factor in where they want to locate their church to help reach that goal. Just like a person who has a goal to make his/her life more comfortable by moving closer to work, a potentially multiracial church must consider how its location can make it harder or easier to attract members of different racial groups. A church's decision to move or, sometimes more importantly, not to move has a powerful effect on whether the church can meet its goal of developing a multiracial environment.

THE FLIGHT FROM AMERICA'S INNER CITIES

The amount of residential segregation in America is both amazing and discouraging. According to the 1980 census, the average African American who lives in the North lives in a neighborhood that is, on average, 80 percent black, and those who live in the South live in neighborhoods that are, on average, 70 percent black.[1] This level of segregation has not improved much over the last twenty years. The segregation of Hispanics and Asians is less than that of blacks, but all people of color with a lower socioeconomic status experience significant residential racial segregation. This residential segregation illustrates the degree of racial alienation that plagues our society and shows why multiracial churches are so hard to create.

The phenomenon called white flight—European Americans leaving neighborhoods when people of color move into the community—helps explain the current level of residential racial segregation in our nation. Andrew Hacker argues that if African Americans move into a neighborhood in sufficient numbers to make up at least 8 percent of the population, then whites will move from that neighborhood until it becomes devoid of European Americans.[2] Research has consistently shown that whites desire to live in integrated neighborhoods less than racial minorities.[3]

People of color understand that whites are less willing to live in integrated neighborhoods than they are. This understanding helps explain why white flight is insulting to people of color. They accurately perceive the rejection being communicated to them by the unwillingness of whites to be their neighbors. Predominantly white Christian churches frequently follow whites in their flight out of the neighborhoods of racial minorities. For example, Michael Pocock and Joseph Henriques note that a pastor told them how he handled the emerging racial diversity in his neighborhood: he raised funds to build a bigger church farther away from racial minorities. It was his second move for that same reason.[4] This type of movement is common. A drive through the inner cities of our minority communities reveals a plethora of church buildings once owned by white congregations that now house minority congregations. Predominantly white churches that left the inner city are in effect rejecting racial minorities, and people of color are rightly turned off by this rejection.

THE REACTION OF MULTIRACIAL CHURCHES TO WHITE FLIGHT

We have something of a paradox: on the one hand, Americans are more willing to drive a good distance to attend a church they like. The rise of megachurches illustrates this point. Most megachurches attract a large population of people that drives ten, twenty or even thirty miles to go to church.[5] Yet even these megachurches often fail to become multiracial. This is especially the case with megachurches located in white suburbs. When I visited megachurches in the suburbs I found that such churches tend to attract a smattering of people of color, but generally whites make up more than 90 percent of the congregation. Given the relative willingness of Americans to drive a significant distance to church and the fact that these megachurches are obviously successful in attracting middle-class Americans, why do they not become multiracial? Clearly this paradox shows that location is important for multiracial churches.

It is fairly clear that many of these predominantly white megachurches have fled the inner cities much like other white institutions. Racial minorities, especially African Americans, are aware of the effects of white flight. They recognize how the fleeing of capital and resources from their communities has harmed their neighborhoods. They perceive predominantly white suburban churches as places not welcoming to them. A person of color can assert that if the white members of that church wanted to interact with racial minorities then they would not move the church away from communities of color.

Of course, such a belief may not be fair to a particular congregation. Many suburban churches were started in those suburbs and thus never "left" racial minorities. However, these racial minorities are accurate in reacting to a general trend among white Americans to reject them through racial segregation. This mistrust is not limited to African Americans, even though they are the racial minority group most likely to live in a segregated neighborhood. Latino Americans are likely to attend the Demographic multiracial churches,[6] which happen to be the type of multiracial churches most likely to incorporate the principle of location. The willingness of a predominately white church to remain in a neighborhood as racial minorities move into that community is an important factor for multiple racial minority groups.

The mistrust of Christians of color toward white suburban churches is not directly linked to specific actions of a particular church, but to the larger structural implications of white flight and neighborhood segregation. A church that does decide to move into a white suburban area, regardless of the reason for this move, will find it incredibly difficult to become multiracial for some time to come. Such a move identifies this church as one that intends to minister primarily to European Americans for the foreseeable future.

I encountered several predominantly white churches that intentionally decided against moving to predominantly white suburbs so that the church could minister to the racial minorities moving into the neighborhood. One church fired the pastor because he did not want to stay in the transitional neighborhood and hired a pastor who had a vision for a multiracial ministry. Had that church moved, I am very certain that it would not enjoy a multiracial ministry today. In another church the leadership decided to convert an old defense plant into a church rather than erect a new church building in the suburbs. The pastor of this church was very talented and would have undoubtedly developed a large suburban church if they had moved. Yet by staying in the area this church was able to develop a very large racially diverse congregation. In both cases the churches transitioned from monoracial to multiracial churches.

CAN WE HAVE MULTIRACIAL CHURCHES IN THE SUBURBS?

What encouragement can I offer churches that want to become multiracial but are already located in neighborhoods that are not integrated? The most obvious possibility for such churches is to move to a more integrated area. A pastor of a multiracial church that developed because of moving into the inner city noted that if you have a heart for a multiracial church then the first thing I would do is come and live in the city and begin to work in the urban city.... I think that if you have a heart for an interracial church, then you need to go to an interracial community. And that's why I moved the ministry, because on the west side you've still got some Italians, you've got a great Hispanic community there. On the east side it's primarily black. So we're right in the middle of everybody, you know. Let those come who want to come.

Obviously, most churches do not value having a multiracial congregation enough to make such a radical decision. But if a church does have enough of a desire to create a multiracial congregation, then such a move may be what is necessary. However, short of moving, other factors should also be taken into consideration.

First, it should be noted that it is possible to find multiracial churches in segregated neighborhoods. These churches often had to work harder to maintain their multiracial character, but some of them were successful nonetheless. However, most of the multiracial churches found in the Lilly study were in predominantly minority or multiracial neighborhoods.[7] Rarely were multiracial churches found in predominantly white suburban neighborhoods.[8] It seems that it is easier to persuade some European Americans to come to churches in the inner city than it is to persuade a significant number of racial minorities to attend churches in white suburbs.[9] This illustrates the degree of alienation that racial minorities have experienced because of residential segregation in America.

Second, as America becomes more multiracial, Christian churches may soon find themselves in integrated neighborhoods. With the exception of African Americans, middle-class racial minorities tend to integrate in middle-class white neighborhoods. Since this is true, the challenge for predominantly white churches will be how to make these minorities feel comfortable within their churches. Predominantly white churches in suburban neighborhoods who today are unable to attract racial minorities into their church services might find racial minorities more easily in the coming years. The key for these churches is to remain in their neighborhoods when more people of color move into them and then to utilize the other principles in this book to make their churches more racially inclusive.

MOVING TO BECOME MULTIRACIAL

If a suburban church desires to wait until the neighborhood becomes more multiracial, it can be a long time before this occurs. This leaves such a church with the first option I mentioned. The church can move in an attempt to locate in a multiracial neighborhood. This does not necessarily mean that the entire church has to be relocated for the congregation to initiate a multiracial ministry. For example, some suburban churches started ministries in the inner city that eventually turned into multiracial churches. Each time this occurred with the churches in the Lilly study, it was a predominantly white church that sent some of its European American members to minister to people of color. In other churches the entire congregation moved to allow the congregation to become more multiracial. Whether it is the entire church or an attempted new church plant with some of the current church members, moving to a more racially diverse area of a city is always a viable option for the development of a multiracial congregation.

It may not be enough, however, to merely move into a different section of town. Some towns have so little racial diversity that they lack any neighborhood with a sufficient number of minority group members to allow a racially diverse congregation to develop. For example, I have lived in a small town that had less than one hundred African Americans and relatively few Hispanic Americans. It was not possible for the church I attended to relocate to an area of the city that would allow the church to become multiracial. On the other hand, if a ministry is extremely committed to becoming multiracial, perhaps that ministry will not be able to stay in such a town. This is the observation of one pastor of a multiracial church:

> [I] think one of the solutions is that more Christians need to move out of the South and the Midwest and move into the new cosmopolitan global centers and give their lives to see the new church emerge, and that's where it's really difficult because ... if someone in Des Moines comes up and says I want to establish the cutting edge Christian church of the future, I want to deal with this issue of multiculturalism, I want to be a part of seeing the church emerge within this poor ... global environment, tell me how to do it in Des Moines, you go—MOVE!

While I do not endorse such a radical position, it is worth noting that a ministry may be limited in how racially diverse it can become simply because of the racial makeup of the city. Churches in small towns that are heavily white may have to accept the fact that they cannot become multiracial. However, there are other cultural dimensions (class, ethnicity, political orientation) in which such a church might introduce diversity into its congregation.

Nevertheless, I would caution church leaders to not be too quick to give up on finding members of different races to minister to. When I lived in Wisconsin I had several white friends who lived in Madison who often told me that there was not a predominantly black neighborhood in Madison because not many blacks lived there. Yet one day my wife found a shop that had African and African American artwork. When she drove around in the area of the city around that shop she discovered that it was a predominantly black neighborhood. My well-meaning white friends had been sheltered from the existence of this African American area of town. The percentage of blacks in Madison is rather low, yet it is high enough for the dynamics of residential segregation to occur. A predominantly white church that wants to become multiracial can minister in this neighborhood to produce a racially diverse ministry. Given this experience, I suggest that you fully investigate any possibility of racial diversity within your city before giving up the effort to locate people of different races. There may be other hidden populations (e.g., ethnic refugees, Native Americans) that can integrate your church.

CONCLUSION

Location is an important factor for many multiracial churches. The phenomenon of white flight suggests that whites in suburban churches may not want racially diverse congregations. Churches in those suburbs that want to become multiracial have difficult decisions to make. Such churches may attempt church plants into the more multiracial areas of the city, which can become racially diverse churches, or they can move themselves. Some predominately white churches attempt to use bus ministries to the inner city to attract people of color into the churches. Yet very little evidence shows that churches can persuade racial minorities to come to predominately white suburban churches merely by providing busing that targets racial minorities in the inner cities.[10] It may be the case that people of color require those suburban churches to make more of a commitment to them than a ministry that sends people into their community just to pick them up for church. However, I did notice that predominately white churches with members willing to commit to ministering to people of color in neighborhoods of color on a consistent basis had more success creating multiracial ministries in those minority communities. Thus, people of color may desire the commitment of a church that is willing to move or at least the commitment of some members of that church to come into their neighborhood for worship instead of shipping them out of their own neighborhood.

Churches in neighborhoods that are closer to people of different races have an easier time becoming multiracial. However, they will have to fight off the urge to move as members of different racial groups come into the neighborhood, and they will have to make plans for reaching out to these groups. The desire to move can be driven by the hope of obtaining the financial rewards or social status of having a potential suburban megachurch. But if multiracial churches are the churches of the future, then such hopes should not totally dictate a decision to move since churches in multiracial neighborhoods are in a much better position to become racially integrated than suburban churches.

Finally, this chapter on location may have the most relevance to new church plants. It is much more difficult to move an already established church into a racially diverse community than it is to start a new church in that community. Those who are responsible for making decisions about where to plant new churches would do well to consider locating these new churches in areas that give them the possibility of developing a multiracial ministry. Such planning can help Christians to create the racially diverse churches that will be necessary for twenty-first-century Christianity.

12

ADAPTABILITY

It was a strict fundamentalist church. It only accepted the King James Version of the Bible. Generally, a rigid, conservative theology goes along with a very conservative political/social philosophy, and this church was no exception to that rule. However, this church did differ from most other fundamentalist churches in a critical way. This formerly almost all-white church had developed a ministry to blacks that created a multiracial atmosphere. Among many ultraconservative white Christians, interracial dating and marriage—particularly to blacks—is taboo. But because of the multiracial makeup of this church, the members of this congregation departed from some of the racist, antimiscegenation teachings adopted by many other fundamental churches. It is just plain hard to teach that blacks and whites should not mix when you have blacks and whites developing friendships and relationships in your congregation. Over time, the pastor of the church moved from a position of opposition to interracial romantic unions to one of acceptance without endorsement. In fact, there were a few white-black couples in the congregation when I visited this church. This is especially noteworthy since one of the things I noticed about the highly segregated city where this church was located was the dearth of multiracial couples. (When I went out to dinner with my white co-researcher and we sat together, we repeatedly received stares from other diners. And he is a man! I do not know what would have happened if I had been eating with a white woman.) The pastor's previous attitude toward interracial romantic relationships could go unchallenged when he was leading an almost exclusively white congregation in this highly segregated city (even though this attitude was racist), but his former perspective toward exogamy became incongruous in a multiracial Christian environment and was discarded. Previous political and social perspectives of this minister underwent revisions in light of the new realities brought by a multiracial atmosphere.

We must anticipate the changes a multiracial congregation will bring and, if possible, prepare for them. As the story above suggests, we must be ready to adapt and change previous ideas and practices that may work in a monoracial setting but not in a multiracial one. While the above story involves the rather extreme idea of antimiscegenation that had to be altered, those in multiracial churches are likely to find other ways in which they will have to make adjustments. The Bible talks about anticipating the cost of discipleship. Jesus warns that if a king with ten thousand soldiers has to go to war against another king with twenty thousand soldiers then the king would be wise to consider if his ten thousand can defend the kingdom against the twenty thousand coming against it (Luke 14:31-33).

Yet we cannot anticipate every possible new situation that the emerging multiracial environment will bring. Anyone who has been a Christian for any length of time knows that our life in Christ has brought both unexpected joys and unanticipated challenges. While it is wise to try to anticipate what our new life as Christ's disciples will bring, it is impossible to be ready for everything coming our way. Likewise, it is important to anticipate the changes that becoming multiracial will bring to the life of a church. Many of these changes will be very joyful, but we must also be ready for the challenges that multiracial congregations bring.

There is a temptation among some Christians to expect those who join their church to accept the culture of the church rather than for the current church members to make new changes to accommodate the newcomers. Naturally a church cannot adapt to every desire brought by newcomers. But it is important that churches learn from newcomers and make some adaptations to facilitate their entrance into the church. The move of many churches to a contemporary worship service to accommodate the musical tastes of the younger cohort is one nonracial example of such adaptation. An emerging multiracial church cannot completely overhaul itself to accommodate new racial groups, but the members would do well to learn how to adapt to these new attendees if they want to keep them. It is too much to expect members of the new racial group to completely leave their old culture at the church door without the church making some accommodations for them as well.

In this chapter I will explore this quality of adaptability by bringing up important issues to anticipate in new multiracial settings. Though impossible to predict everything that can happen as a church makes the transition from being monoracial to multiracial, one can plan for some issues. Ministries that desire to become multiracial are wise to consider these and should be ready to think differently than they have in the past.

ISSUES THAT REQUIRE ADAPTABILITY

Pointing out a few of the issues that a church may have to adapt to may help leaders think of other issues that can arise. One such issue is the potential language barrier. If a multiracial church begins to attract Hispanics and Asians, especially first-generation immigrants, then language will be an issue of concern for church leaders. Many Americans today hold an attitude that immigrants should simply learn English and adapt to our society. No one denies that learning

English is essential. But an "English only" ideology toward Asian and Hispanic immigrants neither shows them respect nor appreciates their culture. Furthermore, it is unrealistic to expect first-generation immigrants to instantly learn English as soon as they come across our borders. Once we understand the difficulty of living in a culture when unfamiliar with just the basic language, we will better sympathize with the plight of these individuals.

To help first-generation Latino and Asian Americans, multiracial churches need to find ways to compensate for the problems that language barriers can bring. Some churches compensated by creating ministries and worship services in the native tongue of these immigrants. Even if the first-generation immigrants did not fully participate with the other church members, it was hoped that over time the children of the immigrants will join the main body of the church, helping integrate the congregation.[1] Other churches used equipment that allows people who are not fluent in English to hear the sermon in their own language. Translation and assistive listening systems are available to allow a speaker of a foreign language to translate the sermon for immigrants.[2] Some churches used English as a Second Language programs to serve these populations. While I would also suggest augmenting such programs with other techniques, clearly using these programs indicates some desire to meet the needs of non-English speakers.

Finally, most of the multiracial churches that included large populations of either Asians or Hispanics used non-English language in signs, programs, décor and other features that made the experience for these groups more enjoyable. Even if a multiracial church was attracting Asians or Hispanics who were educated and fluent in English, the use of Spanish or Asian languages showed respect for the other cultures as well as helping attract those without a full grasp of English.

Another important issue multiracial churches will have to deal with is the presence of interracial couples and multiracial families. While it is tempting to think that in the twenty-first century, concerns about interracial families are a thing of the past, unfortunately, this is not the case. As I indicated in the opening story to this chapter, one of the pastors of a multiracial church had to rethink his earlier opposition to such relationships because his church had begun to attract interracial couples. There are still many Christians who hold on to old notions of racial purity and do not accept interracial marriages. A pastor related to me that, while reaching out to his community, he encountered six or seven interracial families who were rejected by other churches because their families were multiracial.

More than once, I encountered individuals who were fairly comfortable with the fact that the church was multiracial, and perhaps were even working to maintain the multiracial makeup of the church, but were very uncomfortable with the new multiracial families now present. While I have no direct evidence for this, I suspect that one of the major reasons why some people leave multiracial churches is because of the latent prejudice they still have against interracial families. In an interracial church, prejudice has a way of revealing itself at inappropriate times. While no pastor or church leader can completely remove the hidden racism within many Christians, they can do their best to prepare the congregation for the multiracial families that the church may attract. I recently edited a book with my wife called *Just Don't Marry One,* which can offer some guidance in this area.[3]

Another important issue that must be addressed in a multiracial church is prevention of the estrangement of the numerical minority groups in the church. In most multiracial churches there are racial groups that are larger and more powerful than other racial groups. Those in the smaller groups may leave the church. If enough members of these groups leave the church then that multiracial church can slowly turn into a monoracial church as those in the majority become an even larger percentage of the church.

Research by a couple of my colleagues, Brad Christenson and Michael Emerson, helps illustrate this problem.[4] They conducted research on a multiracial church where Filipinos made up a little more than half the church. All other racial groups were "minority" groups within that church.[5] Their research indicated that minority groups in the multiracial church were less likely than the Filipino church members to develop close personal friendships within their church and even to have friends of their own race in the church. The research also showed that Filipinos were more likely than non-Filipinos to have church members as their closest friends. This has important implications since if the numerical majority group (Filipinos) were more likely to have members of their own church as their closest friends, then those in the minority group, the non-Filipinos, will be more likely to feel isolated from other church members and to eventually leave the church. If enough non-Filipinos left the church then this congregation could become a predominantly Filipino congregation instead of a multiracial church.

This research suggests that leaders in multiracial churches have to learn to culturally adapt to the numerical minority groups entering the church. One of the issues that came up in the church that Christenson and Emerson studied was the fact that Filipino culture tends to give deference to older individuals. This made it harder for non-Filipinos with more egalitarian relationships with older individuals. This cultural difference easily led to misunderstandings between Filipinos and non-Filipinos in their interaction with the elderly. I am not arguing that Filipino culture should be abandoned. But to maintain their multiracial atmosphere, the leaders of this church may eventually have to find ways to produce a socially comfortable environment for those not socialized to give deference to older individuals. Members of the majority culture in a multiracial church have to alter the church's social environment so that minority group members are comfortable in the church. The cultural norms of the numerical majority cannot be so inflexible that people who were not socialized in that racial culture will be constantly uncomfortable.

It is natural for us to believe that the culture we learned as a child is the "right" or even the only way culture should be organized. But such an attitude makes it more difficult to make the cultural adjustments necessary to produce a more comfortable social environment for minority groups. To adapt to the influx of a new racial group it becomes important for the leaders of a multiracial church to learn about the new groups coming in. In fact, the pastors of multiracial churches showed an interest in learning about other racial groups. Here are some answers given to the question, "As pastor of a multiracial church, what do you still feel you need information about?"

> I would say more specific information regarding the various needs of the various cultures that we are actually reaching out to because they vary with different people.

I wish I understood Asian cultures better because there are a number of different Asian cultures within 10-12 minutes of us that are harder to understand right now because they are a little bit newer here and are also first-generation immigrants.

To minister to the Africans means taking a great deal of time, spending a lot of time eating and talking. It also takes time for the different groups to trust each other, to feel at home in this space.

These three quotes show pastors who are trying to find ways to learn about cultures that differ from their own and who realized the importance of learning about other racial groups. Perhaps exposure to members of other racial groups helped these pastors know that they were socialized differently, not better or worse, than other members of their congregation. To minister to members of different races they understood the importance of learning about other racial groups.

There are a variety of ways leaders of multiracial churches can learn about the cultures of different racial groups. One of the easiest ways is to simply sit down and talk with church members that are of a different race. These members are valuable sources of cultural knowledge, which these leaders can tap. While leaders must be careful not to make any person the expert on an entire race of people, listening to those members with a nonjudgmental attitude is a surefire way to expand one's cultural knowledge. (Of course, it is also important that nonleader members of different races in the church talk to each other as well.)

A second way a church leader can learn about different racial cultures is by conducting research on these groups. Books and websites on African Americans, Latino Americans, Native Americans, Asian Americans and other racial groups abound today.[6] Books on crosscultural communication can also give such pastors great help. While such resources often do not directly address issues of social culture, they do provide helpful perspectives and insights.

Third, a leader can learn about the racial cultures of other groups by attending cultural events. Juneteenth, Cinco de Mayo and Chinese New Year are just some of the events a pastor can attend to learn about other racial groups. Furthermore, many cities today have museums dedicated to minority racial groups (e.g., a black history museum). Attending such cultural events and activities will not only allow church leaders to learn more about other racial groups, but also communicate cultural acceptance to the minority members of the church and challenge the numerical majority members to become more culturally accommodating as well.

A major benefit of learning about different racial cultures is that this information will enhance the ability of the pastors to minister to the members of different cultures. A pastor of a triracial (white, Hispanic, Asian) multiracial church illustrates this point:

> One of the things that people mistakenly think is that Asian and Latin cultures are identical in terms of being communal, but actually Asian cultures are communal and Latin cultures are familial. And that's a very subtle and significant difference. And so when you have people in Asian culture who make that decision that they are a part of the community, there is a high level of trust. The only way that you get a high level of trust in many Latin cultures is actually from the family. And so when you're the nondirect leader you don't have a lot of trust naturally in that setting. You have to be the director in the family, almost like a personal pastor. And so you have different rhythms of how influence goes in the cultures, and then in the Caucasian culture it is different on top of that because it's really the Caucasian's standards or beliefs that the Bible teaches democracy. And so Caucasians feel like they have to be processed one by one, every individual.

Clearly the knowledge that this pastor has accumulated because of the different racial groups in his church aided his knowledge of how to relate differently to

European, Hispanic or Asian Americans. While he was not asked how he obtained this knowledge (this pastor was Hispanic so his knowledge of Latinos likely came from his own upbringing), personal experience has taught me that such learning about other cultures does not come without effort.

Since people in the numerical minority groups have a harder time developing friendships within the church, they pay a higher price for the racial diversity of the church. But a positive finding of the Christenson and Emerson study is that the members of these minority groups valued being in a multiracial environment so much that they were willing to stay at the church despite the high price they paid.[7] Thus, minority members who join a multiracial church possess a high commitment to living an integrated life. A wise church leader can use the high commitment level of the numerical minority group members in their church—and hopefully also of the majority—to help make the adaptations necessary for the multiracial church to thrive.

Another issue potential leaders of multiracial churches may have to think about is how they approach secular political or social issues. As Emerson and Smith note, white and black Christians tend to have different perspectives on racialized social issues.[8] White Christians tend to develop what they call a "freewill individualist" perspective, which means that white

Christians blame individuals for their own problems. African American Christians tend to develop a more structuralist perspective, an outlook in which black Christians focus on the way racism has affected social structures (e.g., government, businesses) when accounting for the problems individuals face.

To illustrate this difference, imagine that a white and a black Christian both come upon a poor minority single mother of several children on welfare. The typical white conservative Christian response sees this situation as a result of the poor sexual values of the woman and the father(s) of the children, her unwillingness to find employment and her personal expectation that the government should take care of her. A typical black Christian response may acknowledge that these factors are important, but black Christians most likely also perceive this situation as a result of a welfare system that does not provide the type of support that they need (e.g., childcare, job training), the lack of a transportation system to take them to the better jobs in the suburbs and the low opportunity costs they incur for having children because of their lack of economic opportunities. Black Christians see these structural problems linked to the persistence of institutional racism in our society, while white Christians are unlikely to make any attributions to racism unless that expression of racism is overt and personal (e.g., an employer who states that blacks will not be hired).

Of course, I cannot do justice to this difference in one paragraph, and I recommend that readers pick up Emerson and Smith's book to gain a more complete explanation. But this difference in how white and black Christians understand racism continues to erect a barrier to racial understanding in the Christian church. Leaders of multiracial churches had better be prepared to deal with these different political/social attitudes. When there is open communication between members of different races in a church setting, some of these differences will surface.

A white leader of a multiracial church related how he came to understand that racial minorities understood social issues differently than he did:

> I'll give an example of something I really learned. During the Rodney King riots ... the white people called it the Rodney King riots, the black people called it the civil unrest, and that's all the difference in the world. And we had a great discussion about that one night.... As a little guy, I was brought up to respect police and if I ever had a problem I could go to a policeman and they would be my friend. I found out that the black people in this area who were raising their children have NOT had that kind of experience with policemen; they've had a different kind of experience. They teach their children not to go to the policeman and if you do, don't say anything to them because

you don't know what they are going to do. A VERY different awareness.

Clearly the police represent something quite different to him as a white man than to African Americans. The police meant security to him because of his physical appearance. Many blacks, on the other hand, do not see the police as a solution to their problems but as an extension of the racism within society itself. African Americans know a great deal about instances of the misuse of police power about which many European Americans are ignorant, and so African Americans are more wary of police officers. I am not arguing that the blacks have the right perspective about the police and whites are totally wrong. The correct answer is probably somewhere in the middle. But bringing people of different races into a church brings contrasting perspectives of U.S. society into that church, and leaders of the church need to prepare to handle these differences.[9] Leaders of multiracial churches can continue to believe social perspectives that are part of their own racial culture but they will have to learn how to live with those who have perspectives different from their own.

A final caveat on this last point is needed. Often people of a minority group race who joined the church early did so because they were either drawn to the culture of the numerical majority group (e.g., whites who enjoy Latino culture and music may join a predominantly Hispanic church) or they were alienated from their own racial culture (e.g., blacks who reject elements within African American culture may join a predominantly white church).[10] These individuals tend to agree with the social perspectives of the majority culture of the church. However, individuals of that race who later join the church do not always have the same perspectives as the earlier group. If the church wishes to continue to reach out to members of that race, then the leaders of the group should not make the mistake of believing that the individuals of different races who joined earlier represent the perspectives of everyone in that race.

LEADERSHIP AND ADAPTABILITY

Leaders of a church will play a critical role in helping members of their church adapt to the new multiracial reality. They can fulfill this role in key ways. First, these leaders can aid the congregation's adaptability through efforts to educate the members and prepare them for a multiracial church. Before a pastor takes intentional steps to create a multiracial congregation, that pastor would do well to preach, teach and encourage members of the congregation to get ready for the new norms and issues that will arise because of racial integration.

Second, it is important that the leadership of the church spend time anticipating which issues the congregation may have to adapt to. It is impossible for anyone to completely anticipate all of the new challenges that creating or maintaining a multiracial church will bring, but a wise leader will be ready to deal with unexpected ministerial challenges. This chapter presents just a few of the potential struggles that may arise when a church becomes multiracial. I strongly recommend that leaders of multiracial churches look over these issues and use them as starting points for conversations about what other issues may develop within their racially integrated congregation. Each congregation has unique circumstances and there are many potential issues that can arise to produce special challenges, but time spent attempting to anticipate some of these challenges is time well spent.

Given the important role leadership plays in helping the church become multiracial, it is not surprising that Leadership multiracial churches are the ones most likely to incorporate the principle of adaptability.[11] Multiracial leadership can aid a congregation in anticipating problems since individuals from different racial groups can bring out perspectives not perceived by members of the numerical majority. Such racial diversity in the leadership also makes it easier for the leadership team to educate members of the congregation since each major racial group in the congregation can have someone on the leadership staff help them understand the new challenges. Thus, one of the ways to become more adaptable is to incorporate the techniques of diverse leadership discussed in chapter seven.

CONCLUSION

Any major change in our lives will require effort to adapt; some adaptations will be expected and some unexpected. Even positive changes create such a demand. Going to college was a wonderful experience in my life. Some of the adaptations I had to make for college, such as increasing the time I had to commit to academic study, were expected. Other adaptations I had to make, such as dealing with loud dorm neighbors, were unexpected. But overall the experience of going to college was positive, and I am very happy that I went to school. By remaining adaptable and teachable to the new situations that arose during my schooling, I was able to make the most of this positive experience. Likewise, becoming a multiracial church can be an overall positive experience. But to make the most of this experience you must be ready to be flexible and adaptable to the new and sometimes unexpected challenges that will come your way.

This chapter is not meant to be an exhaustive list of potential adaptations. The purpose of this chapter is to warn church leaders that it is important to anticipate new tests that racial integration brings. Once a church leader has been sufficiently warned, then it is the responsibility of that leader to develop a mindset flexible enough to deal with the new challenges. Those who desire an integrated congregation will have to decide what they cannot change and where they can be flexible in changing. All of the churches in the Lilly study had to make some adjustments, even if minor ones, in their attitudes or practices in order to maintain their racial integration. Thus, it is better to be ready to make changes than to be locked into an inflexible attitude.

13

CONCLUSION

This book has not been written with the idea that multiracial churches are a panacea to all of the racial problems in the United States. Multiracial churches do offer our Christian community in particular and the United States in general certain benefits that justify the effort needed to generate and sustain these churches. But we have had centuries of racial abuse in our nation, and a few years of worshiping together is not going to eliminate all of the effects of that abuse. While racially integrated churches offer an opportunity to have the type of meaningful interracial interaction that has been missing throughout much of our history, it is foolish to believe that multiracial churches will solve all of our racial problems. Furthermore, not all multiracial churches are very effective in producing racial healing or in retaining members of the numerical minority. Some of the multiracial churches discovered in the Lilly study merely reproduced many of the values that have led to racial alienation. Others seemed to create few of the social attitudes that may help bring about racial reconciliation.

Since not all multiracial churches are fruitful for producing racial healing, I would like to use the last few pages in this book to explore how multiracial churches can be organized to maximize the positive benefits they offer. For the bulk of the book I have been drawing on the research conducted with the Lilly study to inform church leaders of the best ways to develop or maintain a multiracial congregation. But in the next section I will rely less on research and more on my own values and thoughts concerning multiracial congregations. So take the advice in this chapter for what it is worth, the ranting of this one sociologist, rather than the results of pure research.

ASSIMILATION OR PLURALISM

In chapter three I explored the arguments of cultural pluralists who fear the eradication of minority group cultures because of racially integrated institutions. Given their concerns, a question can be legitimately asked: can multiracial churches smother the culture of racial minorities? The answer is *yes.* As I investigated multiracial congregations, I saw some that were able to maintain a Eurocentric culture. These churches can be criticized as attempts to force racial minorities to lose their culture and conform to the cultural wishes of majority group members. Most successful multiracial churches tend to adapt the cultures of many different racial groups, but I would be negligent to ignore the fact that Eurocentric multiracial churches are possible. Since such an

Anglo-conformist type of assimilation is possible, the concerns of cultural pluralists deserve to be addressed.

It is important for leaders of multiracial churches to intentionally work to prevent the type of assimilation that disregards the racial culture of people from the nonmajority groups. In addition, if assimilation does occur, it is important for it to occur in a way that incorporates the cultural aspects of the different races in the church—so that all racial groups will gain a certain amount of respect. Many of the steps recommended in this book, such as diverse leadership and inclusive worship, are measures that can be used to recognize the value of different cultures. It is vital to take these steps if we want to assure those in the minority that they will be respected. Such steps will minimize the alienation of numerically smaller racial groups and enable them to communicate their concerns to the rest of the church. I believe that this will not only decrease the possibility of losing members in the numerical minority but also increase the possibility that the church will make real efforts toward racial reconciliation. Even churches that consist predominantly of minority group members but want to include whites in order to become multiracial should not expect whites to merely adopt the culture of the racial minority groups. The most valuable type of multiracial church is one where different racial cultures can be expressed.

ALLOW FOR BOTH MULTIRACIAL AND MONORACIAL SUPPORT GROUPS

Communication between different racial groups is critical. Too often multiracial churches do not create the social structures within their organization that allow for the multiracial communication necessary for racial reconciliation. Chapter three documented how such communication was critical for the racial reconciliation that occurred in the ministry of Spencer Perkins and Chris Rice. Leaders of multiracial churches should ask whether their church provides opportunities for people of different races to express their honest feelings about racial issues. Within multiracial Christian settings, there will be people dealing with sins of racism, either within themselves or from others. Interaction in a supportive multiracial community has great value for helping such individuals deal with those sins. Do not make the mistake of believing that once you are in a multiracial church your struggles with racism are over. Monitor for racial segregation within your church so that a true interracial community can develop.

Some multiracial churches make the opposite mistake. They discourage all groups within the church that are not multiracial. However, there is a time and place for monoracial groups. Such groups can allow members of that race to support each other because they understand some of the struggles of the members of that group. This is not unlike the practice of many churches to have sex-segregated groups because they recognize that men and women have different issues to deal with. It would be unhealthy if a church always segregated men from women, but segregation in certain situations makes sense.[1] Likewise, while it would be unhealthy if a multiracial church always segregated by race, some race-specific groups can be useful.

Both multiracial and monoracial support groups can be particularly important in meeting the needs of numerical minority church members. The multiracial communication that comes from integrated support groups helps assure the members of this numerical minority that they will have a voice. The monoracial support groups help them handle issues unique to themselves. Thus, it is vital for multiracial churches to build social structures that help facilitate both multiracial and monoracial support groups.

CONTINUE TO LISTEN TO MEMBERS OF NUMERICAL RACIAL MINORITIES

I pointed out in the last chapter that numerical racial minorities who initially join a church often do so because they are attracted to the racial culture of that church rather than their own racial culture. When a church first becomes multiracial the leaders of that church tend to consult with the members of the numerical minority. But after a church has been multiracial for a while, there is less incentive for these leaders to consult with such individuals as the novelty of being multiracial begins to wear off. There is a natural tendency for these leaders to believe that they already have sufficient knowledge to minister to members of the numerical minority groups. Church leaders assume that the members of the numerical minority group who join the church later will have similar concerns and perspectives to those who joined the church earlier. This assumption is often a mistake.

Members of the numerical minority who join after this first wave often have perspectives and interests that differ from their racial brothers and sisters. Churches that rely on their understanding of the first wave of the numerical minority often unintentionally discourage more members of that racial group from joining the church. In fact, some of the earlier members of the numerical minority may join that church to escape members of their own race, and when the leadership of the church consults them, these individuals often validate the racial status quo. But the later cohorts of that numerical minority group are likely to be individuals who are more willing to shake up that status quo. If the leaders of the church do not listen to this later cohort, they will often lose out on the opportunity to make the alterations that can enable the church to become even more racially diverse.

A major problem that plagues multiracial churches is keeping the members of the numerical minority group from leaving the church. Losing these members robs those churches of the potential for the true integrated Christian fellowship that enhances racial reconciliation. To the degree that multiracial churches are valuable we must think about how we can minister to those in the numerical minority. Those in the numerical majority can easily make their desires known, but those in the numerical minority often have their needs go unnoticed. Thus, leaders of multiracial congregations should pay special attention to the desires and needs of numerical minorities. Efforts to minister to these minorities can come at a cost for those in the majority. Yet if a racially integrated congregation is of value, then it is worth paying that price.

In light of the importance of listening to the numerical minority, multiracial churches cannot become complacent. The leaders of such a church must continue to consult with the members of the numerical minority groups even as new members of that group continue to join the church. This consultation should never end. Individuals in this racial group who join the church later are likely to have suggestions that will help the church attract members of that race who may not be easily predisposed to join a multiracial church.

INCORPORATING BLACKS: A UNIQUE CHALLENGE

I want to go to back to the Lilly data to touch on one more important issue and unique challenge faced by some multiracial churches—the incorporation of blacks into their congregations. I am convinced that African Americans are more difficult to attract into multiracial congregations than other racial groups. There is some evidence that indicates why this may be the case. For example, African Americans face more residential segregation than other racial groups. They are also less likely to marry people of other races than other racial minorities. In another book I have argued that blacks have a more difficult time gaining acceptance in our society than other racial minorities.[2] Given all of these social factors, it is not a surprise that the most common racial configuration of multiracial churches combines whites with Hispanics or Asians. Just as African Americans are less likely to live in racially integrated neighborhoods or to interracially marry, they are also less likely to attend multiracial churches.

If one of the target groups of a potential or actual multiracial church is African Americans, then the leadership of that church should understand that it will be more difficult to attract blacks than to draw Latinos and Asians into the church. The evidence from the Lilly study suggests two areas that such congregations can concentrate upon in an effort to attract African Americans: efforts at finding black clergy or lay leadership and encouragement of discussions of racial issues.

It is possible to be a multiracial church with blacks in the congregation and to have no African Americans in leadership. However, there appears to be a ceiling on the percentage of blacks that will be attracted to such a congregation. In the Lilly data the highest percentage of blacks that attended a church with no black clergy was 33 percent. The highest percentage of whites and Hispanics who were willing to attend churches without members of their own group in leadership was 50 percent.[3] Other measures indicate that multiracial churches that are proactive and intentional in creating racial diversity in leadership had higher percentages of African Americans than other multiracial churches.[4] These trends indicate that representative leadership is especially important for African Americans. The very first thing a ministry that wants to reach out to African Americans should do is to find ways to place blacks in the clergy or lay leadership.

The second issue is allowing for the discussion of racial issues. The Lilly data suggests that multiracial churches that spend considerable time discussing racial issues attract more African Americans than other multiracial churches. If the alienation between African Americans and the rest of society is greater than the alienation faced by other racial minority groups, then discussion of racial issues may be necessary to allow blacks to vent some of the frustration they experience. Because of this alienation, such discussions may also be important to help members of other races understand the unique perspectives of African Americans. It is vital that multiracial churches do not attempt to hide racial issues under the philosophy of "colorblindness." A more healthy and perhaps necessary approach for multiracial churches with relatively high numbers of African Americans is one that creates times and places for members of all racial groups to explore racial issues.

Efforts to discuss racial issues must be intentional as such conversations will not happen automatically and resentment can build up until African Americans begin to leave the church. One of the multiracial churches in the Lilly study had a black woman church member who went to a pastor about a racial concern. The response she received was that racial issues were not to be talked about from the pulpit or at official church functions. If she wanted to talk about the racial problems she saw within the church then she could do so only in a one-on-one conversation with that pastor. She found this unacceptable and left. If this church had allowed her to express her perspective in a more public forum, it could have brought about much-needed dialogue to the members of that church and she likely would have remained in that congregation. It is not surprising that the percentage of blacks in this church remains small, as African Americans seem to need opportunities to express their racial concerns.

LET'S DO IT

I challenge you to become active in turning around the statement that "Sunday morning is the most segregated time of the week." It should have never been this way. While there may be reasons why certain congregations do not integrate racially, I believe that most of God's churches are supposed to be a multiracial kaleidoscope.[5] Every Sunday morning we should encounter those of different races and cultures, learn from them, teach them and then go out into the world to give a visible witness about the diversity of our Christian faith. The fact that this is not the case for most Christians says more about our inability to faithfully follow Christ, who freely gave his healing to Jews and Greeks, rather than about the power of the gospel. It is up to us to begin to bind racial wounds among ourselves so that we can show the rest of our society how our Christian walk can have real relevance to the problems that hinder our country.

How can you get started? In chapter four I suggested the four major paths that multiracial churches can take to become multiracial. If you are the leader of a church and have influence in your congregation, then read this chapter again to think about how you may begin moving on one or more of those paths in the church's ministry. If you are not in a position of authority, then you have two basic choices. You can seek out a church that is multiracial or in the process of becoming multiracial and join that church. Or you can work from within your own church to provide a groundswell of support for a multiracial congregation. The second choice will undoubtedly take more time, but has the benefit that you get to work within established friendships in your church.

If you are a leader within a Christian organization or denomination you can make sure that having racially integrated congregations is a priority within your organization or denomination. The results of the bulk of the research in this book will help you dispense practical advice to others in your organization or denomination. In addition, you can generate multiracial congregations in other creative ways. When possible, you can merge congregations that have different racial groups within a denomination. Short of actually merging, you can provide organizations and forums that encourage different racial groups within your denomination to interact with each other and perhaps build important alliances. It is also an option for some churches to "loan" their members to another church for a year or so. For example, if a predominantly Asian church "loans" some of its members to a white church, then this white church will temporarily be multiracial. This can create a social atmosphere that makes it easier to attract racial minorities, and this temporary multiracial state can become permanent.

I am under no illusion that these are easy steps to take. I personally know the challenge of trying to find a multiracial church and of trying to impart a multiracial vision to members of a monoracial church. But the great difficulty associated with meeting this goal will also bring about tremendous rewards as we in the body of Christ begin to win the victories that multiracial congregations will bring. It will be rewarding because we will see achievements that are beyond the abilities of humans, achievements that can only be obtained through God. We will see an enrichment of our fellowship we never thought possible. We will have the fruits of racial reconciliation at which the non-Christian world will marvel. Those of us who have been involved in racial reconciliation have been challenged for years about the construction of multiracial ministries. Other Christians who have not heard of this challenge as much as we have still know that Christian segregation is wrong.

It is time to put an end to the racial barriers that prevent us from worshiping together. Are you prepared to make the sacrifices necessary to eradicate these obstacles? Come on, brothers and sisters, let's do the hard work necessary to create the multiracial churches we require for the body of Christ and provide the witness of racial healing so desperately needed by our society.

APPENDIX A

HOW THIS RESEARCH WAS CONDUCTED

This section gives a relatively brief explanation of how the research in this book was conducted. Statisticians and methodologists who want a more in-depth explanation of the first three stages of this research are free to contact me or to read a forthcoming book by Michael Emerson with the working title *People of the Dream: Religion and the Quest for Racial Integration.* [1] Those who want more information about the last stage need to contact me directly. In the section below we refers to Dr. Emerson (the principal researcher of the grant), Dr. Karen Chai (another coresearcher) and myself.

STEP ONE: NATIONAL TELEPHONE SURVEY

This stage consisted of a national random-digit dialing telephone survey with a probability sample. After enough whites were interviewed we then surveyed only blacks, Hispanics and Asians until we had enough racial minorities to make valid cross-racial comparisons. When we had enough of these racial minority groups, we surveyed a nonprobability sample of people who went to racially integrated churches so that we would have enough multiracial church attendees to make useful comparisons. We found these people by calling churches in several randomly chosen metropolitan areas and asking the leaders of those congregations if they knew congregations that were multiracial. We contacted those churches and asked for a list of people to call. (Table 1)

Which of the following factors have led to your congregation being multiracial/ethnic?

a.	Just happened, people began showing up and staying	
b.	Congregation moved to a new location in an attempt to become multiracial/ethnic	(.301)
c.	Congregation moved to a new location for another reason	(.216)
d.	Neighborhood became more racially or ethnically diverse	(.535)
e.	Movement of God	(.33)
f.	Existing clergy developed multiracial/ethnic vision	(.631)
g.	New clergy came with multiracial/ethnic vision	(.62)
h.	Lay leadership developed multiracial/ethnic vision	(.632)
i.	Clergy urged congregation to make a deliberate effort	(.779)
j.	Congregation members themselves decided to make a deliberate effort	(.434)
k.	Part of the congregation's evangelism plan	(.785)
l.	Part of the congregation's social outreach program	(.441)
m.	Members married interracially/ethnically	(.539)
n.	Friendship circles expanded multiracially/ethnically	(.776)
o.	New student population	(.131)
p.	Original members left church	(.267)
q.	Changed worship styles	(.136)
r.	Offered worship services in different languages	(.212)

Table 1. Question Used to Determine How Churches Became Multiracial

The people interviewed were asked which church they attended and that gave us our sample of churches. This sample was then used to construct a relatively random list of churches with a nonprobability oversample of multiracial churches. These are the churches utilized for the remaining steps in the project.

STEP TWO: NATIONAL CONGREGATION MAIL SURVEY

A nationwide mail survey was conducted with the Catholic and Protestant congregations found in the survey in step one. The questionnaire was sent to the churches targeted for this study, asking them to have someone knowledgeable about the church answer questions about the demographic, social, institutional, philosophical and theological characteristics of the congregation. Reminder postcards were twice sent to churches that had not responded to the questionnaire. Most of the time (65.8 percent) the head pastor/priest of the church answered the questionnaire, but sometimes associate ministers, church secretaries, lay leaders or other individuals answered the questionnaire.

On the questionnaire we asked the leaders of these churches to check all of the reasons why they originally became multiracial. Table 1 lists the question we used to assess these reasons. From this question

I was able to conduct a factor analysis,[2] which indicated that there were four basic explanations for the origin of multiracial churches. With the exception of the first explanation ("Just happened, people began showing up and staying") all of the variables were assigned to one of the four basic explanations generated by the factor analysis. This analysis also produced a value for each variable by which it can be weighed into the group to which it is assigned. This technique allows a variable that has a stronger correlation with a given factor to be more powerful in predicting that factor for a specific church.[3] After examining each group of variables within each factor, I choose names for the factors: Leadership, Evangelism, Demographic and Network. It is my belief that these terms best conceptualized what I see happening with the multiracial origin of these churches. For a better explanation about these types, see chapter four.[4]

The rest of the questionnaire provided answers for other questions regarding multiracial churches, such as how likely are they to grow, their gender makeup, their theological orientation and so on.

STEP THREE: VISITING THE MULTIRACIAL CHURCHES

We also conducted field research in four metropolitan areas. One area was chosen from each of the four major geographical regions in the United States (West, South, Northeast, Northcentral). Care was taken to make sure that different sizes of metropolitan areas were chosen (from a medium size city of about 50,000 people to a megalopolis of several million people). Once these areas were chosen, we used the information gained from the mail questionnaire to locate potential multiracial churches in that area and to contact the senior clergy of that congregation. If this person could not be immediately reached then generally an administrative assistant would be asked to forward the request. If the church refused to cooperate, then other multiracial churches were approached. Ideally, at least four multiracial churches and two monoracial churches would be selected for each metropolitan area, but in the two smaller areas, only three cooperative multiracial churches could be found. To compensate for this shortcoming, five multiracial churches were studied in the largest metropolitan area. Fifteen multiracial churches (and one multiethnic church that was not multiracial) were studied at this step of the study.[5] The information gained by the previous mail questionnaire helped insure that the multiracial churches selected were diverse in their theological orientation, racial identity of the head clergy and size of congregation.

After these churches were selected, we flew to those cities and interviewed members of the clergy and lay leadership of those churches. We tried to interview eight church members of each multiracial congregation and four church members of each monoracial congregation, although we did not always reach this goal. With a couple of exceptions, the senior clergy at all of the multiracial congregations were interviewed. At a few of the larger multiracial congregations other clergy were interviewed too. We attended the worship services of these churches and investigated secondary documents to understand the social backgrounds of the congregations.

What was of most interest for this current book were our interviews of the clergy. Table 2 lists the questions we asked those clergy members. These questions were used to examine the joys, problems and lessons learned by those who were leading multiracial churches. While I did not personally interview every clergy member, we had the interviews transcribed, which allowed me to read what each one said. The quotes that I utilized in this book came from those interviews.

After I had completed all of the visits to these churches, I begin to conceptualize why these churches were able to maintain their multiracial mix. Some of my conclusions came directly from the clergy interviews. Some of my conclusions came from my analysis of the social conditions under which the churches were established. Some of my conclusions came from observations made while attending worship services and church-sponsored events. From these conclusions I developed the seven general principles that I discussed in the last half of the book.

STEP FOUR: FOLLOW-UP MAILOUT SURVEY

After coming up with these seven principles, I decided to learn more about them with a follow-up survey. At this stage I was greatly aided by the work of Roger Grothe who attended an early presentation in which I discussed these principles. He constructed a very useful questionnaire that allowed me to measure these seven principles in current multiracial churches. It was a short instrument that I sent out to the multiracial churches that answered the original questionnaire. This questionnaire grouped together the statements related to each of the principles. Table 3 gives the list of questions for each of the principles discussed in this book. (Table 2)

Questions for All Church Pastors
1. Can you tell me about your background?
   a. How did you end up as a pastor/priest here?
2. How did this church get started?
3. What are the biggest current goals of this church?
   a. Spiritual goals?
   b. Organizational goals?
4. What is the biggest accomplishment of this church?
5. What is the biggest failing of this church?

226

6. Would you describe your members as generally mature in their faith/commitment to the church [for Catholics], babies in their faith/commitment to the church, or some mix?

7. In the next ten years, what do you think the most important issue or issues facing this church will be?

8. What are the top moral or social issues that churches ought to address?

Table 2 (a). Questions Used in the Pastoral Interviews

Questions for Multiracial Church Pastors

1. How did this church become multiracial?

2. What, if anything, do you do to make sure that the church stays multiracial?

3. What would other pastors who know you say about you and your church?

4. Do you have any racial issues in your church? How do you deal with racial issues within the church?

5. Have you changed anything about your church because of the different people attending? Have you experienced any difficulties or blessings because you are multiracial?

6. Do you think your church should be multiracial? Why? Does it matter?

7. Theologically, do you think churches should be multiracial, uniracial, doesn't matter, or depends on the situation? Why?

8. If others felt God was calling their church to be multiracial, but didn't know how to go about getting started, what advice would you give them?

9. What have you learned by being part of this? What did you wish you knew that you now know? What, if anything, do you feel like you still need information about?

Table 2 (b). Questions Used in the Pastoral Interviews

After receiving the answers from the multiracial churches, I ran statistical tests to see if these statements are strongly correlated to each other, which can indicate if there is a common factor that links these statements together. With one exception (the questions dealing with location)[6] the statements for each of the principles were highly correlated to each other. I am now comfortable making the assumption that those questions capture the dimension I intended to measure.

The follow-up survey also gave me an excellent chance to identify which of the seven principles that each church utilized and implemented in the life of their congregation. From this data I was able to construct indexes for each principle, and then I could use correlation and regression analysis to assess which principle is linked to which characteristic of multiracial churches. This analysis allowed me to see how each principle influences our understanding of multiracial churches. For example, because the original questionnaire documents the percentage of African Americans in multiracial churches, I can use the measures on this follow-up questionnaire to see if any of the seven principles are correlated with having a high percentage of blacks in the church. This result led to my observation in chapter thirteen that a racially diverse leadership is correlated with a relatively higher percentage of African Americans.

Other such observations in this book have come from similar analysis of this data.

CONCLUSION

It would be arrogant for me to argue that this research is the last academic word on multiracial churches. There are several shortcomings in this research that future empirical work can help correct. However, before this research was conducted there was no systematic research on racially integrated congregations, and thus the Lilly study has been a tremendous initial attempt to understand the dynamics of multiracial churches. If you want to further explore some of the data gathered in this study, please contact me at <dryancey@racialreconciliation .com>. (Table 3)

After carefully reading each survey item, please indicate the extent to which you agree with each statement (as it pertains to your church). 1-strongly disagree 2-disagree 3-neither agree or disagree 4-agree 5-strongly agree

Inclusive Worship
• Different racial/cultural styles of music are often incorporated within the same service.
• From week to week, the music typically varies from one racial/cultural style to another.
• From week to week, the preaching typically varies from one racial/cultural style to another.
• The preaching style is not associated with any one racial/cultural group within the congregation.
• The music style is not associated with any one racial/cultural group within the congregation.

Inclusive Worship

- The interior decoration of the church (e.g., artwork, banners, pictures, images of Christ, etc.) is not associated with any one racial/cultural group within the congregation.

Table 3 (a). Questions Used in the Follow-Up Survey to Capture the Characteristics of Multiracial Congregations

Diverse Leadership

- The church is proactive and intentional when it comes to the racial diversity of staff and lay leadership.
- Leaders who are not members of the majority race in the church are visible in worship and other corporate gatherings.
- There is a proportionate number of staff and lay leaders who are not members of the majority race in the church.
- The views and perspectives of different racial/ethnic groups influence the decision-making of the head clergy in the church.

Table 3 (b). Questions Used in the Follow-Up Survey to Capture the Characteristics of Multiracial Congregations

Overarching Goal

- Major ministry goals within the church are tied to becoming more multiracial.
- There is a sense of purpose and vision that is easily recognized by individuals within the church.
- Church members and regular attendees perceive becoming a multiracial church as being an essential element leading to the achievement of other goals (e.g., community service, evangelism, etc.)
- The congregation is energized and hopeful when it comes to becoming a more multiracial church.

Table 3 (c). Questions Used in the Follow-Up Survey to Capture the Characteristics of Multiracial Congregations

Personal Skills

- Members and regular attenders are patient with one another in matters relating to race and have developed the ability to handle setbacks with kindness, wisdom and even laughter.

230

Personal Skills

- Church members and regular attenders are sensitive to the needs of others—especially those that are racially different from them.
- There is openness to empowering people who are not members of the majority race to lead and direct the affairs of the church.
- The leaders of the church demonstrate the ability to communicate, understand and empathize with people of different races and cultures.

Table 3 (d). Questions Used in the Follow-Up Survey to Capture the Characteristics of Multiracial Congregations

Location

- The church is known for communicating a feeling of acceptance and openness to people of all races within the community.
- The church is physically located in an area of marked diversity.
- An increasing number of regular church attendees tend to come from the immediate community.

Table 3 (e). Questions Used in the Follow-Up Survey to Capture the Characteristics of Multiracial Congregations

Intentionality

- The congregation expresses their desire to become a more multiracial church through thoughts, words and actions.
- In spite of struggles and setbacks, church leaders remain committed to the goal of becoming a more multiracial church.
- Considerable time is spent talking about issues related to becoming a more multiracial church throughout the year.
- Church leaders have formally set becoming a multiracial church as one of the top-level church goals.

Table 3 (f). Questions Used in the Follow-Up Survey to Capture the Characteristics of Multiracial Congregations

Adaptability

- The staff and lay leadership team spends time anticipating potential obstacles to becoming a more multiracial church.

Adaptability

- The staff and lay leadership team has set goals for educating the congregation and preparing them for participation in a more multiracial church.

- Generally, the congregation embraces new racial/cultural norms and practices (e.g., worship styles, interracial marriage, biracial adoption, different views of time, etc.).

- Church leaders demonstrate flexibility in handling the challenges that are associated with becoming a multiracial church.

Table 3 (g). Questions Used in the Follow-Up Survey to Capture the Characteristics of Multiracial Congregations

APPENDIX B

USEFUL WEBSITES

Antioch Global Network <www.antiochglobalnetwork.org>. This is an organization of churches committed to multiracial ministry. This network is based out of Antioch Bible Church in Seattle, Washington, but churches from all over the nation support this network. The network generally sponsors a conference every year to help equip those who want to do multiracial ministry.

BridgeLeader Network <www.bridgeleader.com>. A network of churches and other organizations headed up by David Anderson, pastor of BridgeLeader Community Church located in Columbia, Maryland. This network seeks to provide resources to multiracial ministries. It is an excellent organization for multiracial churches located in the Northeast.

Crossroads Bible College <www.crossroads.edu>. Although more and more colleges have attempted to include more multicultural elements in their curriculum, I have found none as dedicated to multiracial ministry as Crossroads Bible College. One of the primary missions of this college is the development of leaders for multiracial urban ministries. Thus, this college is much more intentional about preparing leaders of multiracial ministries than other Christian undergraduate schools.

Erace Foundation <www.erace.com>. Geared toward helping younger Christians (ages 15-25) deal with issues of racial reconciliation, this website might provide valuable resources if the church is attempting to reach out to younger Christians of different races.

Multicultural Ministry <www.mcmweb.org>. Multicultural Ministry can show you the how-tos and guide you through the process of transitioning your church from a monocultural to a multicultural, multilingual local church ministry. It is a ministry headed up by Arturo Lucero, who specializes as a consultant for helping churches deal with issues of racial diversity.

Multiracial Congregations Project <www.congregations.info>. This website contains the home page of the project that generated the research for this book, which was sponsored by Lilly Endowment. It has a resource page, discussion lists and a search engine for multiracial churches. Churches that are multiracial are welcome to register at this site so that those of us who want to find a multiracial church can do so more easily. This website also lists resources for multiracial churches.

Reconciliation Consulting <www.racialreconciliation.com>. This is my own website through which I can be contacted. At this website I run the consulting business Reconciliation Consulting, as well as sell books and other resources that are helpful for a multiracial ministry. Come and visit me.

APPENDIX C

DETERMINING THE TYPE OF MULTIRACIAL CHURCH OF A CONGREGATION

The purpose of this section is to allow readers to determine the type of multiracial church to which they belong. Chapter four discussed a typology I created based upon how a church became multiracial. Understanding how a church became multiracial is important since the origin of the racially integrated nature of a church is related to other characteristics of that church. Comprehending this origin can have important implications for how a church can retain its racial diversity or become more racially diverse.

Table 1 of appendix A lists the questions used to determine the origin of the multiracial nature of a church. To use this table for your own church, merely go through each factor and honestly answer yes or no on whether that factor describes an important reason why your church has become multiracial. You can answer yes to as many factors as you think are appropriate, but remember that this tool will only be useful if you are as honest as possible. It may be helpful to make copies of this table and have other people who know about the multiracial origin of the

236

church answer the questions as well as yourself, and then accept only the answers that show up on a majority of the responses. It is unimportant whether your church was begun as a multiracial church or converted to becoming multiracial after being monoracial for a while since even churches that start out multiracial have reasons why they started out multiracial.

I recommend that you answer the question in table 1 before reading any further to prevent any bias in your answers.

Once you have answered the question in table 1, you can use the following scale to help determine the type of multiracial church you belong to:

- responses e, f, h, i, j and r are linked to Leadership multiracial churches;

- responses c, k and l are linked to Evangelism multiracial churches;

- responses d, g and p are linked to Demographic multiracial churches;

- responses b, m, n, o and q are linked to Network multiracial churches;

- response a was not related to any of the four types; you can drop it from further analysis.

For most churches, this calculation will make pretty clear which type of church they are. Many will answer yes to three or four statements in one of the types while no more than once in the statements of any of the other types. However, it must be remembered that these different types of churches are not mutually exclusive. That means that a church can be, to differing degrees, both an Evangelical and a Network multiracial church. So do not be surprised if your church scores highly in more than one factor. If you feel that it is very important to assert one of these types above the other three types, then another procedure will enable you to do so. Once again, I do not believe that the most important lesson to learn from this exercise is determining exactly which type of church one has; it is also valuable to know if the origin of your multiracial congregation is linked to two or three different sources.

Nevertheless, if the knowledge gained from using the scale above is not sufficient, then you can perform the following calculations. Beside each response is a number within parentheses. If you have determined that this particular response accounts for the multiracial origin of your congregation, write this number down underneath the corresponding type of church. Then add all of the numbers for that type together. For example, if you have determined that interracial marriages (.539), a new student population (.131) and the expansion of interracial friendships (.776) help account for the multiracial nature of your church, then you have a total score of 1.446 (.539+.131+.776=1.446) under the Network type of multiracial churches. If none of the other types score above 1.446 then you can assert that your church's multiracial origins conform more to the social networks pattern than to any of the other sources of origin, although this does not mean that these other sources did not play an important role in helping you become multiracial. Following the steps in this paragraph is not necessary and should only be done if you feel it is vital to determine which one type best explains the multiracial origin of your church.

Once you have determined which type(s) describes your church, I suggest that you reread chapter four with special attention to the type(s) that pertains to your particular congregation. I also suggest that you look through the book for times when I discuss the particular type(s) of your church for more possible insight.

Perhaps the greatest asset of this work is that it can enable a church to discover areas that need strengthening in their multiracial ministry. It is quite important to assess which of the seven principles discussed in this book your congregation is doing well and which you need to work on. This can be done by examining the qualitative content of each principle and then exploring specific ways that a church/ministry can improve its implementation of this principle.

If you desire to do a superficial assessment of your church's ability to implement these seven principles, then go to table 3 and honestly answer each of the statements using the scale provided there. Notice that the statements are placed under each of the seven principles. Add the numbers under each principle together. After finding each principle's total, divide that total by the number of statements under each principle to determine the average. Wherever your average score for a principle is low, that is a principle you need to work on.

For example, there are four statements under the principle of diverse leadership. Let us assume that you slightly disagree that your church is proactive and intentional when it comes the racial diversity of the staff and lay leadership (a score of 2), strongly agree that leaders who are not part of the member race are visible in worship and other corporate gatherings (a score of 5), and strongly disagree that there is a proportionate number of staff and lay leaders who are not members of the majority race in the church (a score of 1) and that the views and perspectives of different racial/ethnic groups influence the decision making of the head clergy in the church (a score of 1). This (5+2+1+1) adds up to nine. Dividing the nine by the number of dimensions assessed gives us 9/4 or 2.25. I suggest that any principle for which you do not score at least 3.5 is a principle that can definitely use some work. Thus, a multiracial church with the scores below 3.5 should consider how to develop racially diverse leadership.

This leads to the second step: how to improve the implementation of these principles. It is clear that the statements themselves imply suggestions on how you might work on these principles. In the example above, the members of this church would do well to take note that the head clergy lacks input from racial minority groups and that there is not a proportional number of members of the minority group in the staff and lay leadership. To a lesser degree, there is also a lack of an intentional effort to recruit staff and lay leaders of the numerical minority groups. These are specific areas where this hypothetical church can improve its ability to incorporate racially diverse leadership into its ministry.

While this assessment provides an excellent preliminary analysis of your church, it is still limited by the fact that this analysis is being conducted by members of the church, who will suffer from a strong bias to support their church. It must also be noted that any instrument I put into this book had to be generic. Your church will have unique aspects that have to be taken into account. If you are extremely interested in making the changes necessary to create or maintain a multiracial mixture in your unique situation, it would be quite beneficial to get outside expert analysis. This analysis can be especially valuable in helping craft a plan that meets the particular needs of your church. The best place to gain such in-depth analysis is through the ministry of Roger Grothe at the Institute for Biblical Reconciliation. He has developed materials to aid the multiracial development of Christian churches and can be contacted at <grotherogerw@msn.com> or 651-681-9357.

NOTES

Chapter 1: Introduction

[1] Compared to the degree of educational and occupational segregation that existed in the early part of the twentieth century, particularly in the Jim Crow South, there is dramatically more racial integration today. For evidence of the decreasing educational segregation, see Nancy St. John, *School Desegregation: Outcomes for Children* (New York: Wiley, 1975).

[2] Mark Chavez, "National Congregations Study," machine-readable file (Tucson, Ariz.: Department of Sociology, University of Arizona, 1999).

[3] Thomas Pettigrew and Joanne Martin argue that when minority groups reach 20 percent of an organizational population then the groups have reached a "critical mass." They contend that when racial minorities are in numbers smaller than 20 percent they can be clustered into small low-status groups within the organization. But according to Pettigrew and Martin, 20 percent is a large enough percentage to allow minorities to be filtered throughout the entire organization. This observation legitimates the use of 20 percent as a cut-off point ("Shaping the Organizational Context for Black American Inclusion," *Journal of Social Issues* 43 [1987]:41-78).

[4] George Yancey, "Racial Attitudes: Differences in Racial Attitudes of People Attending Multiracial

and Uniracial Congregations," *Research in the Social Scientific Study of Religion* 12 (2001):185-206.

[5] The fact that most Americans are mistaken about this notion of physical differences does not mean that racial distinctions are unimportant. In the appendix to George Yancey and Sherelyn Yancey, *Just Don't Marry One: Interracial Dating, Marriages and Parenting* (Valley Forge, Penn.: Judson Press, 2002), I have illustrated that racial distinctions are based more upon our social perception than actual physical differences between members of different races. For example, even though many think of blacks as having darker skin than whites, clearly not all blacks are darker than all whites. Differences between blacks and whites are not based on a strict scientific measure of these physical differences, but on the fact that people perceive blacks and whites to be physically different from each other. The power of this perception is what creates the social conditions that have established the racial conflict we see in our society.

[6] Some of these churches also contained smaller racial groups such as Native Americans and Middle Easterners. But none of these groups were large enough in any given church to make up a significant percentage of that church. This is not to argue that there are not multiracial churches that have a large percentage of Native

Americans or Middle Easterners, but that we simply were not able to find such a church in our limited sample.

[7] "Multiracial Congregations and Their People," grant #1998-1384-000, was sponsored by the Lilly Endowment (1999-2001).

[8] For the most part I will report on the results of correlational analysis in these notes. However, with many of these findings I also utilized more sophisticated techniques such as multiple regression and factor analysis.

Chapter 2: Multiracial Churches: Past and Present

[1] Jordan D. Winthrop, *White over Black* (Baltimore: Penguin, 1968).

[2] For a more comprehensive treatment of the history of multiracial churches please read Curtiss DeYoung, Michael Emerson, George Yancey and Karen Chai, *United by Faith* (Oxford: Oxford University Press, 2003).

[3] W . Harrison Daniel, "Virginia Baptists and the Negro in the Early Republic," *Virginia Magazine of History and Biography* 80 (1972):60-69.

[4] David M. Reimers, *White Protestantism and the Negro* (New York: Oxford University Press, 1965), pp.74-76.

[5] George E. Haynes, "Are Christians Finding Interracial Fellowship within the Church?" *Federal Council Bulletin* 13 (October 1930):11, 26.

[6] Millard Fuller, *The Theology of the Hammer* (Macon, Ga.: Smyth & Helwys, 1994), pp.2-3.

[7] It is of interest to note that the Samaritans were actually a mixed-race people, a result of Hebrews having intermingled with the Cuthaeans after the Assyrian conquest of the Hebrews. The Jewish resentment of the Samaritans was precisely because of their assumed ambiguous racial status and the threat they offered to notions of Jewish purity (2 Kings 17:24-41). Given this reality it becomes obvious how Jordan developed lessons about race relations from biblical stories that contained Samaritans.

[8] Karen J. Chai, "Competing for the Second Generation: English-Language Ministry at a Korean Protestant Church," in *Gathering in Diaspora: Religious Communities and the New Immigration,* ed. R. Stephen Warner and Judith G. Wittner (Philadelphia: Temple University Press, 1998), pp.295-331.

[9] Nancy A. Denton and Douglas S. Massey, "Residential Segregation of Blacks, Hispanics, and Asians by Socioeconomic Status and Generation," *Social Science Quarterly* 69 (1988):797-817.

[10] For a more complete Christian critique of color-blindness, see my article "Color Blindness, Political Correctness or Racial Reconciliation: Christian Ethics and Race," *Christian Ethics Today* 35, no.7 (2001):15-17.

246

[11] For a more comprehensive explanation of the effects of historical residential segregation on the contemporary life chances of blacks, I recommend Douglas Massey and Nancy Denton, *American Apartheid: Segregation and the Making of the Underclass* (Cambridge, Mass.: Harvard University Press, 1993).

[12] Joy Kinnon, "DWB: What's Behind the Wave of Attacks on Black Motorists?" *Ebony* 54, no.11 (1999): 62-65; David A. Harris, "Driving While Black: Racial Profiling on our Nation's Highway," *An American Civil Liberties Union Special Report* (1999); Kit R. Roane, "A Risky Trip Through 'White Man's Pass,'" *U.S. News & World Report* 130, no.15 (2001):24.

[13] Leslie Carr, *Color-Blind Racism* (Thousand Oaks, Calif.: Sage Publications, 1997); Joe R. Feagin, *Racist America: Roots, Current Realities and Future Reparations* (New York: Routledge, 2000); Randell N. Robinson, *The Debt: What America Owes to Blacks* (New York: E.P. Dutton, 2001); Vincent N. Parrillo, *Stranger to These Shores: Race and Ethnic Relations in the United States* (Boston: Allyn & Bacon, 2000); John E. Farley, *Majority-Minority Relations* (Upper Saddle River, N.J.: Prentice Hall, 2000).

Chapter 3: Should We Have Multiracial Churches?

[1] The founders of this church growth movement may be Donald A. McGavran and Winfield C. Arn. In their book *Ten Steps for Church Growth* (San Francisco: Harper & Row, 1977), they argue that while racial segregation is wrong, churches that are composed of several different nationalities do not tend to grow or multiply. From this perspective church growth must be sacrificed if a congregation wants to become multiracial.

[2] The single most elaborate and powerful work that supports this model can be seen in the book by C. Peter Wagner, *Our Kind of People: The Ethnical Dimensions of Church Growth in America* (Atlanta: John Knox Press, 1979). Wagner coined the phrase "homogeneous unit principle," which is the concept that culturally homogenous churches are the ones that grow the fastest. In a later book of his, *The Healthy Church: Avoiding and Curing the 9 Diseases That Can Afflict Any Church* (Ventura, Calif.: Regal, 1996), he softens his stance some-what, but still contends that it is a mistake to place too much focus on attracting people from a variety of different cultural groups.

[3] This saying is commonly attributed to Captain Richard Pratt, who used the Carlisle School

248

for Indian Students to attempt to "civilize" Native Americans. While Pratt's philosophy may be considered progressive for its time, today it is commonly recognized as a form of cultural genocide.

[4] William Cenkner, ed. *The Multicultural Church: A New Landscape in U.S. Theologies* (New York: Paulist, 1996).

[5] James H. Cone, *Black Theology and Black Power* (Maryknoll, N.Y.: Orbis, 1969); Albert B. Cleage Jr., *Black Christian Nationalism* (New York: Morrow, 1972).

[6] Eldin Villafañe, *The Liberating Spirit: Toward an Hispanic American Pentecostal Social Ethic* (Lanham, Md.: University Press of America, 1995); Arturo J. Bañuelas, "U.S. Hispanic Theology: An Initial Assessment," in *Mestizo Christianity: Theology from the Latino Perspective,* ed. Arturo J. Bañuelas (Maryknoll, N.Y.: Orbis, 1995), pp.55-82; Virgil P. Elizondo, "*Mestizaje* as a Locus of Theological Reflection," in *Mestizo Christianity: Theology from the Latino Perspective,* ed. Arturo J. Bañuelas (Maryknoll, N.Y.: Orbis, 1995), pp.7-27.

[7] For example, pretend that we have two churches and we want to see which church will grow faster over time. In one church we have only 10 members and in the other church we have 1,000 members. If our first church picks up only three members in the course of a

year—perhaps a mother, father and their child join the church—then the growth rate of that church will be 30 percent. In order for the other church to grow 30 percent, they would have to pick up 300 members in a single year's time. That would be quite a task. Thus it is relatively easy for small groups to obtain tremendous growth rates that are deceiving. But the growth rates of the small congregations are likely to eventually slow down as the congregations get bigger and the addition of a few members does not translate to a huge growth rate increase.

[8]   The unweighted average number of adults in multiracial churches was 711 and the average number of total members of the church (adults and children) was 965. The unweighted average number of adults in monoracial churches was 586 and the average number of total members of the church (adults and children) was 810.

[9]   I used a regression technique to control for other possible factors such as size of city, location of the church in the city (downtown, suburb, etc.), attitudes of church toward ecumenicalism, whether the church had a traditional or modern outlook, age of the leaders of the church and whether the church was Protestant or Catholic. Despite all of these controls I still found evidence that multiracial churches had a stronger propensity to grow than monoracial churches.

[10]   Of course, not all Christians are equally likely to desire a multiracial environment. There are important demographic and social differences between Christians who attended multiracial churches and other Christians. Correlations of whether a Christian attends a multiracial church and variables that measured sex, age, income, education, political attitude, region of country and whether the respondent lived in a large city or suburb indicated that Christians who were higher educated, lived in the West and lived in a large city were more likely to attend multiracial churches. Clearly, pastors in the Western part of the United States who want to attract educated individuals in large cities should be extremely willing to originate multiracial churches. However, establishing multiracial churches is valuable for other church leaders as well. Correlation analysis with data from the phone survey indicates that multiracial church attendees attend church at a much higher rate than other Christians (r=.196). This suggests that there is a stronger commitment to the church attendance among people who attend multiracial churches, making such Americans an extremely attractive target population for church leaders.

[11]   To use a nonracially based example of this statement, I personally witnessed a church

split that overtly seemed to be about worship styles but in fact was a conflict between age cohorts. The younger cohort sensed that the older cohort resisted allowing them to participate in the direction of the church and this was manifested in an argument about the type of worship music used. The older cohort disliked the more contemporary praise songs that were used, while the younger cohort saw this music as an overture to their culture. This power struggle led to the firing of the music minister for not playing enough traditional hymns. As a result of this struggle, I saw the exodus of most of the younger church members.

[12]   The only issue where there was statistically significant evidence that multiracial churches have more conflict than monoracial churches was conflict over the behavior of the members of the church.

[13]   Research that suggests that multiracial churches are more likely to adopt a structuralist approach to social issues (which is more in keeping with a philosophy of African American Christianity), rather than an Eurocentric individualistic approach to social issues, can be seen in a paper I presented at the 2001 American Sociological Association meeting in Anaheim, California, entitled "Effects of Attendance at Multiracial Churches on the Individu-

alism of European-American and African-American Christians."

[14] George Yancey, "An Examination of the Effects of Residential and Church Integration on Racial Attitudes of Whites," *Sociological Perspectives* 42, no.2 (1999):279-304.

[15] While I have yet to find information in the 2000 census about the number of interracial families in America today, this census data does indicate that 2.4 percent (6,826,228 individuals) of all Americans marked more than one race on the census. Since multiracial individuals come from interracial unions, it may be argued that about the same percentage of families are multiracial in the United States. This is not a trivial number, as multiracial individuals outnumber the number of Native Americans in our country and are two-thirds the size of the Asian American population. Since American Indians and Asians are populations that have often warranted the attention of Christians, so too should Christians fashion ministries for multiracial families

[16] To find lists of such organizations, I suggest searching the following websites: Interracial Voice <http://www.webcom.com/~intvoice/add_site.html>; Interracial Haven <http://users2.ev1.net/~crusader/irhaven/irsites.html> or The Multiracial Activist <http://www.multiracial.com>.

[17] Spencer Perkins and Chris Rice, *More Than Equals* (Downers Grove, Ill.: InterVarsity Press, 1993); Glen Kehrein and Raleigh Washington, *Breaking Down the Walls* (Chicago: Moody Press, 1993); and Jefferson Edwards, *Purging Racism from Christianity* (Grand Rapids, Mich.: Zondervan, 1996).

[18] George Yancey, *Beyond Black and White: Reflections on Racial Reconciliation* (Grand Rapids, Mich.: Baker, 1996); "Color Blindness, Political Correctness, or Racial Reconciliation: Christian Ethics and Race," *Christian Ethics Today* 35, no.7 (2001):15-17; "Reconciliation Theology: How a Christian Ethic Tackles the Problem of Racism," Christian Scholar's Review 17, no.1 (2003):93-108.

[19] For a more complete analysis of the Christian philosophy of racial reconciliation, see my article "Reconciliation Theology."

[20] Michael Cassidy, *The Passing Summer: A South African's Response to White Fear, Black Anger, and the Politics of Love* (Ventura, Calif.: Regal, 1989), p.267; Andrew Sung Park, *Racial Conflict and Healing: An Asian-American Perspective* (Maryknoll, N.Y.: Orbis, 1996), p.139.

[21] Douglas Massey and Nancy Denton, *American Apartheid: Segregation and the Making of the Underclass* (Cambridge, Mass.: Harvard University Press, 1993).

[22]   According to Mary R. Jackman and Marie Crane, less than 10 percent of all whites can name a black that is a good friend ("'Some of My Best Friends Are Black...': Interracial Friendships and White Racial Attitudes," *Public Opinion Quarterly* 50[1986]:459-86).

[23]   Rachel F. Moran points out that there is a resegregation of education institutions occurring due to people choosing to send their kids to same-race schools. She argues that because this segregation is by individuals' choice instead of legal means that there is little we can do to stem this process by formal measures (*Interracial Intimacy: The Regulation of Race of Romance* [Chicago: University of Chicago Press, 2001]).

[24]   This is particularly the case since such proponents tend to recognize that historically an evangelical form of Christianity has supported imperialism and the subjugation of minority racial group cultures.

[25]   Perkins and Rice, *More Than Equals,* p.132.

[26]   Ibid.

[27]   Ibid., p.137.

[28]   Kehrein and Washington, *Breaking Down the Walls,* p.131; Perkins and Rice, *More Than Equals,* p.238.

[29] In the remainder of the book I will quote pastors or church leaders from the Lilly study. Unless I indicate otherwise, the reader can assume that any of the remaining quotes in the book come from this source.

[30] Howard Clark Kee, *Who Are the People of God? Early Christian Models of Community* (New Haven, Conn.: Yale University Press, 1995); Curtiss Paul DeYoung, *Coming Together: The Bible's Message in an Age of Diversity* (Valley Forge, Penn.: Judson Press, 1995).

[31] For example, during the course of our research the Lilly team attempted to locate multiracial churches in smaller cities. We randomly picked thirty nonmetropolitan areas and called the churches in those areas to see if we could locate any multiracial churches. We only found one nonmetropolitan multiracial church. While cultural segregation undoubtedly played a role in the lack of multiracial churches in these small towns, it is likely that a lack of racial diversity was also a factor. It is improbable that churches located in towns with little racial diversity would be able to become multiracial. Given such a social reality, it seems reasonable that such churches would not

place a high priority upon developing an extensive multiracial ministry.

Chapter 4: Types of Multiracial Churches

[1] I used a technique called factor analysis to construct these four types of churches. This technique allowed me to see whether the same churches gave similar explanations for why they became multiracial. For example, this factor analysis revealed that churches that stated they became multiracial because it was the vision of the lay leadership also tended to indicate that they became multiracial because it was the vision of the existing clergy. This allowed me to group these explanations with others to form the notion of Leadership multiracial churches. Other such groupings helped establish the other types of multiracial churches as well.

[2] Correlation analysis with an index of four charismatic practices (speaking in tongues, shouting "Amen," dancing for joy and being "slain in the Spirit") indicated a significant correlation between churches with the characteristics of Leadership multiracial churches (see the preceding note for how these characteristics were assessed through factor analysis) and these practices (r=.226), but a significant relationship was not found with any of the other types of multiracial churches.

[3]   Of the ten churches from the mailout that I was able to identify distinctly as an Evangelism multiracial churches, nine of them condemned homosexuality with a score of a "1" on a 1 to 7 scale in which lower numbers indicated less support for homosexuality.

[4]   About a third of the churches identified as Demographic multiracial churches were Catholic. This compares to the fact that only about 20 percent of the churches identified as Leadership or Evangelism multiracial churches were Catholic, and only about 12 percent of the churches identified as Network multiracial churches were Catholic.

[5]   Among Protestant churches I found positive but nonsignificant correlations between measures of political liberalism, theological liberalism and ecumenicalism with the tendency of a multiracial church to be a Demographic multiracial church. The relatively small number of multiracial churches that were mainline in orientation (there were only eleven mainline Protestant multiracial churches in the sample) might account for the nonsignificance of these findings.

[6]   According to weighted data, over 90 percent of the churches that were labeled as Network multiracial churches have grown over the past five years. In comparison, 70 percent of the Evangelism, 55 percent of the Leadership and

about 58 percent of the Demographic multiracial churches have grown over the past five years.

[7]   In fact, interracial marriages as an explanation of why a church becomes multiracial loaded heavily on the Network factor. So it is not surprising that the variable of whether interracial marriages helped create a multiracial church is powerfully correlated to churches with the characteristics of Network multiracial churches (r=.644).

Chapter 6: Inclusive Worship

[1]   I make this assertion based on the questionnaire sent out in the fourth stage of this project. Correlations of different types of worship (music, preaching, décor, etc.) showed that measurements of a diversity of music styles were correlated more heavily to a general dimension of inclusive worship than measurements of other types of worship. For a more complete and technical definition of how such correlations can load heavily onto a given dimension or factor you may want to read Jae-On Kim and Charles W. Mueller, *Introduction to Factor Analysis: What It Is and How to Do It* (Beverly Hills, Calif.: Sage Publications, 1978).

[2]   Herbert M. Carson, *Hallelujah! Christian Worship* (Welwyn, England: Evangelical Press, 1980), p.7.

[3]   Louis H. Gunnermann, *Worship: A Course Book for Adults* (Boston: United Church Press, 1966), p.9.

[4]   Alicia Williamson and Sarah Groves, *A Seeking Heart: Rediscovering True Worship* (Birmingham, Ala.: New Hope Publishers, 2001), p.9.

[5]   Robert Morey, *Worship Is All of Life* (Camp Hill, Penn.: Christian Publications, 1984), p.76.

[6]   Bernhard Lang, *Sacred Games: A History of Christian Worship* (New Haven, Conn.: Yale University Press, 1997), p.1.

[7]   This is not to deny the value of learning about the worship of racial groups that are not the target of the church. A worship leader may want to incorporate Spanish songs even though the congregation is predominately white-black. Doing so may show respect to the few Hispanics in the congregation and add to an atmosphere of racial tolerance in the congregation. However, it is my contention that the most immediate need of any church leader should be the racial groups that are the main targets of the church's outreach efforts, and thus the energy needed to learn about other cultures should be directed toward such groups.

[8]   For example, see James Dobson, *The Complete Marriage and Family Home Reference Guide* (Carol Stream, Ill.: Tyndale House, 2000), p.421-22.

[9] Curtiss Paul DeYoung et al. (*United by Faith* [Oxford: Oxford University Press, 2003]) suggest the following books as possible sources for suggestions on cross-cultural worship: Brenda Eatman Aghahowa, *Praising in Black and White: Unity and Diversity in Christian Worship* (Cleveland: United Church Press, 1996); Nancy Tatom Ammerman, *Congregation and Community* (New Brunswick, N.J.: Rutgers University Press, 1997); Kathy Black, *Culturally-Conscious Worship* (St. Louis: Chalice Press, 2000); Kathy Black, *Worship Across Cultures: A Handbook* (Nashville: Abingdon, 1998); Brian K. Blount and Leonora Tubbs Tisdale, *Making Room at the Table: An Invitation to Multicultural Worship* (Louisville, Ky.: Westminster John Knox, 2001); Tee Garlington, "The Eucharist and Racism," in *Ending Racism in the Church,* ed. Susan E. Davies and Sister Paul Teresa Hennessee (Cleveland: United Church Press, 1998), pp.74-80; R. Mark Liebenow, *And Everyone Shall Praise: Resources for Multicultural Worship* (Cleveland: United Church Press, 1999); and Pedrito U. Maynard-Reid, *Diverse Worship: African-American, Caribbean and Hispanic Perspectives* (Downers Grove, Ill.: InterVarsity Press, 2000).

Chapter 7: Diverse Leadership

[1] For example, among monoracial churches that had a white pastor the Lilly data revealed that 87.25 percent of the lay leaders were white, 1.3

percent were black, 1.3 percent were Hispanic and 0.4 percent were Asian. Among multiracial churches that had a white head pastor 51.9 percent of the lay leaders were white, 20.7 percent were black, 13.7 percent were Hispanic and 6 percent were Asian.

[2] Correlation analysis with an index of four measures of diverse leadership that was used in the fourth stage of this project (see table 3 in appendix A) indicated a moderately strong correlation between congregations with the characteristics of Leadership multiracial churches and this index ($r=.369$). Much weaker correlational relationships were found between other types of multiracial churches and this index.

[3] Evidence of this alienation can be seen in the fact that African Americans are less likely to interracially marry (Charles Gallagher, "Racial Redistricting: Expanding the Boundaries of Whiteness," paper presented at the 2002 American Sociological Association meeting, Chicago; and Paul Spickard, *Mixed Blood: Intermarriage and Ethnic Identity in Twentieth Century America* [Madison: University of Wisconsin, 1989]). Evidence that African Americans are less likely to live in a racially integrated community is found in Douglas S. Massey and Nancy A. Denton, *American Apartheid: Segregation and the Making of the Underclass* (Cambridge, Mass.: Harvard University Press, 1993), p.64.

[4] There was a moderate effect (r=.2) between congregations with the characteristics of Leadership multiracial churches and an index of the number of different styles of worship music that these churches employ.

[5] However, this effect might also happen because Leadership multiracial churches tend to be charismatic churches and charismatic churches are more likely to use a variety of worship music.

[6] Those who want to seek out African Americans may want to look at seminaries and Christian colleges that are supported by predominantly black denominations such as C.H. Mason Bible College, Tennessee Fourth Jurisdiction, 250 E. Raines Road, Memphis, TN 38109; Hood Theological Seminary, 800 W. Thomas Street, Salisbury, NC 28144; American Baptist College, 1800 Baptist World Center Drive, Nashville, TN 37207. Support for Hispanic Americans is less focused than for blacks and there are fewer schools aimed at Hispanic Americans. However, the Southern Baptists have started a Bible college/seminary that is aimed at training Hispanic Christian leaders. This institution is Hispanic Baptist Theological School, 8019 S. Pan Am Expressway, San Antonio, TX 78224-1397.

Chapter 8: An Overarching Goal

[1] Credit for this concept belongs to Spencer Perkins and Chris Rice, *More Than Equals: Racial*

Healing for the Sake of the Gospel (Downers Grove Ill.: InterVarsity Press, 1993).

[2]   It is probably not an accident that Leadership multiracial churches are more likely to utilize overarching goals than other types of multiracial churches since it is likely that in these churches the leader has been able to develop an overarching vision for the church that helps the church become racially integrated. Part of the power that these leaders have, which helps them develop a multiracial congregation, can come from this ability to impart such a vision.

[3]   Of course, there were some volunteers of color who helped with the bus ministry, but the vast majority of the volunteers were white.

[4]   Informally I was told that the church had to spend hundreds of thousands of dollars to maintain the buses. While such a figure is plausible I have no way of verifying it.

[5]   It is worth noting that the multiracial churches that were more likely to utilize an overarching goal to help them maintain their racial diversity were also more likely to engage in many of the traditional "social gospel" programs such as providing food, clothing, health care services, etc. than other multiracial churches. This assertion is based upon a significant correlation between an index of the four items in table 3 in appendix A and an index of 15 social gospel types of activities ($r=.267$).

Chapter 9: Intentionality

[1]   I measured the degree to which the churches in this sample adhered to each of the seven principles (see table 3 in appendix A for the items used to measure each of the principles). Of all of the seven principles discussed in this book, I found the two with the highest correlation to each other was intentionality and overarching goals (r=.839). It is clear that churches with overarching goals that are not necessarily directly related to becoming multiracial also take intentional steps to meet those goals and to diversify their congregations.

[2]   Raleigh Washington and Glen Kehrein, *Breaking Down Walls: A Model for Reconciliation in an Age of Racial Strife* (Chicago: Moody Press, 1993), p.127.

[3]   There is a powerful correlation (r=.517) between churches with the characteristics of Leadership multiracial churches and a four-point index of intentionality (see table 3 in appendix A). This tendency may indicate the power of the leaders in Leadership multiracial churches to set goals that are directly related to whether the church will become more multiracial.

[4]   According to the Lilly survey, about 10 percent of all Americans have more friends of different races than their own race, 52 percent have lived in neighborhoods where less than 80 percent of the residents are of their race and

43 percent have attended schools where less than 80 percent of the students are of their race.

[5] I created a scale with the four measures of intentionally that were credited in the fourth step of this research (see table 3 in appendix A). I then compared the multiracial churches that scored high on these four measures with the tendency of a church's attendance to grow, decline or stay the same. I found that there was a mild positive correlation between scoring high on these dimensions of intentionality and the ability of a church to grow (r=.198).

Chapter 10: Personal Skills

[1] The correlation between the percentage of Asian Americans in a multiracial church and their self-reported measure of sensitivity is .236.

[2] There is a mild positive correlation between those churches that tended to have the characteristics of Network multiracial churches and multiracial churches that stated they attempted to empower numerical minority groups (r=.151).

Chapter 11: Location

[1] Douglas S. Massey and Nancy A. Denton, *American Apartheid: Segregation and the Making of the Underclass* (Cambridge, Mass.: Harvard University Press, 1993), p.64.

266

[2]   Andrew Hacker, *Two Nations: Black and White, Separate, Hostile, Unequal* (New York: Ballantine, 1992), p.36.

[3]   Camille Charles Zubrinsky, "Neighborhood Racial-Composition Preferences: Evidence from a Multiethnic Metropolis," *Social Problems* 47, no.3 (2000):379-400; William A. V. Clark, "Residential Preferences and Neighborhood Racial Segregation: A Test of the Schelling Segregation Model," *Demography* 28 (1991):1-19; Maria Krysan and Reynolds Farley, "The Residential Preferences of Blacks: Do They Explain Persistent Segregation?" *Social Forces* 80, no.3 (2002):937-80.

[4]   Michael Pocock and Joseph Henriques, *Cultural Change and Your Church: Helping Your Church Thrive in a Diverse Society* (Grand Rapids, Mich.: Baker, 2002), p.50.

[5]   I have been told that in Chicago people drive forty-five minutes to an hour to attend the megachurch Willow Creek Community Church. Some even commute from Wisconsin and Indiana.

[6]   The Lilly data indicates a mild positive significant correlation (r=.18) between the percentage of Latinos in a multiracial church and whether that church has the characteristics of a Demographic multiracial church.

[7]   In the Lilly study, two-thirds of the multiracial churches were located in neighborhoods

where 50 percent or less of the residents were white.

[8] Over 95 percent of the multiracial churches were located in neighborhoods where 80 percent or less of the residents were white. Since most predominately white suburbs are over 80 percent white, these statistics indicate the rarity of multiracial churches in white suburban neighborhoods. An interesting side note is that I have met two head pastors of multiracial churches in white suburban areas. Both pastors are African American, which may indicate that for multiracial churches in white suburbs to attract people of color, they must clearly exhibit minority leadership.

[9] Maria Krysan and Reynolds Farley suggest that this tendency may be linked to the fear among African Americans that they will have to face the hostility of whites when the move into a pre-dominantly or all-white neighborhood ("The Residential Preferences of Blacks").

[10] Although in fairness, one of the churches mentioned in chapter 8 has experienced moderate success with a bus ministry to African American communities. However, it should be noted that this success has centered on the ability of this church to attract children of color. The church became multiracial because a small fraction of the children

who came to the church remained in the church. Unless a church is willing to undertake the level of commitment of this church (which sends out more than 25 buses every week) and to bring in an extraordinary number of people, that church is unlikely to create a multiracial adult congregation.

Chapter 12: Adaptability

[1]   Art Lucero has advocated this approach for helping monoracial churches incorporate minority groups and has trained leaders of churches for using this method. His ministry can be contacted through his website at <http://www.MCMweb.org>.

[2]   These systems generally include several personal PA units and an Interpreter Control Unit that allows someone to translate from another room for those who are using the PA units.

[3]   George Yancey and Sherelyn Yancey, *Just Don't Marry One: Interracial Dating, Marriages and Parenting* (Valley Forge, Penn.: Judson Press, 2002).

[4]   Brad Christenson and Michael O. Emerson, "The Costs of Diversity in Religious Organizations: An In-Depth Case Study," *Sociology of Religion* (forthcoming).

[5]   By picking a church where Filipino Americans, not European Americans, made up the majority of the church, Christenson and Emerson were able to prevent a confounding of the effects of

societal majority group status and numerical majority group status within the church.

[6]   I did not include European Americans in this list since it is very clear that European culture has a powerful influence in American society. Thus, anyone who lives in the United States for any period of time will begin to understand the cultural norms of European Americans. However, leaders from first-generation ethnic groups may not have an immediate understanding of European American culture and may want to seek out information through friends and other resources including American history/social studies classes at a local community college.

[7]   In fact, Christenson and Emerson located and interviewed four people who left the church. They found that three of the four people who left the church were either looking for or attending another multiracial church.

[8]   Michael Emerson and Christian Smith, *Divided by Faith: Evangelical Religion and the Problem of Race in America* (Oxford: Oxford University Press, 2000).

[9]   Research that I have conducted from the information gathered by the mail survey of this Lilly research suggests that multiracial churches have a less individualistic theological perspective than predominantly white churches. Furthermore, evidence from the phone survey indicates that white members of multiracial churches have less

individualistic attitudes than whites in predominantly white churches. It is plausible
that having members of the racial minorities in a church may influence the social
and racial attitudes of the white members
of the church.

[10]   I credit my co-researchers, Michael Emerson and Karen Chai, for this observation.

[11]   The Lilly data indicated strong positive
correlations between those churches that
tended to have the characteristics of
Leadership multiracial churches and a scale
of four items (see table 3 in appendix A)
that measured how well the church incor-
porated the principle of adaptability
(r=.377).

Chapter 13: Conclusion

[1]   Perhaps the time when I felt that segregation by sex was the most useful was when
I was single and attended Bible studies on
romantic relationships with the opposite sex.
Clearly, being in a group of men allowed for
more honest interaction than would have
been possible if the group were coed.

[2]   George Yancey, *Who Is White? Latinos,
Asians and the New Black/NonBlack Society*
(Boulder, Colo.: Lynne Rienner, 2003).

[3]   For Asian Americans this percentage was
only 40 percent. However, Asian Americans
are a unique case in that there was only one

other multiracial church that had a higher percentage of Asian Americans (50 percent). Asian Americans may be more willing to attend churches without Asian leadership than the 40 percent measure implies.

[4]   There was a positive correlation ($r=.179$) between a self-reported measure of a multiracial congregation's willingness to intentionally seek out diverse leadership and the percentage of African Americans in that congregation.

[5]   A multiracial church may not be advisable if the church is located in a town that does not have many people of color. A multiracial church may also not be advisable if the main targets of the congregation are first-generation immigrants. Such individuals may be undergoing a great deal of culture shock, and a multiracial church may be more than they can handle. For more information on these and other possible exceptions to the responsibility of developing a multiracial church, be sure to read Curtiss Paul DeYoung, Michael Emerson, George Yancey and Karen Chai, *United by Faith* (Oxford: Oxford University Press, 2003).

Appendix A: How This Research Was Conducted

[1]   At the time of publication of this book, the book by Emerson did not yet have a publisher.

[2]   Factor analysis is a statistical technique that basically allows the statistician to see if a single set of variables are relatively independent of one another. If they are not independent of each other then the statistician can assert that there may be underlying factors that dictate a high correlation between the variables. I found four sets of high correlations, which I deduced to be four different types of multiracial churches.

[3]   In the previous notes in this book when I discuss the characteristics of different types of multiracial churches (e.g., chap.4 n.2), I used the results of this analysis to create one of the variables that I used in calculating the correlation. For each church, the weighted value of each explanation in a given factor that was indicated by the church to be important in helping that congregation become multiracial was added together to create a score for each type of multiracial church.

[4]   You may also want to read a more academic treatment of the construction of these four types. This can be found in George Yancey and Michael Emerson, "Integrated Sundays: An Exploratory Study into the Formation of Multiracial

Churches," *Sociological Focus* 36, no.2 (forthcoming).

[5]   These were not the only churches that I utilized in shaping my analysis. I did use knowledge that I gained from other churches that I encountered outside of the Lilly research and from a couple of churches where I performed pretest research work.

[6]   Therefore I did not use the index of Location variables in the analysis reported in the book.

BACK COVER MATERIAL

AS SOCIETY DIVERSIFIES, LOCAL CHURCHES FIND THEM SELVES INTERACTING WITH PEOPLE FROM EVERY TRIBE AND TONGUE.

But not every church is equipped to handle the realities of ethnic and racial diversity in its congregational life. Sociologist George Yancey's pioneering research on multiracial churches offers key principles for church leaders wanting to minister to people from a variety of racial and cultural backgrounds. Insights from real-life congregations provide concrete examples of how churches can welcome people of all heritages, giving them a sense of ownership and partnership in the life of the church.

Based on data from a landmark Lilly Endowment study of multiracial churches across America, this volume offers insights and implications for church leadership, worship styles, conflict resolution and much more. Here is an essential resource for pastors and church leaders committed to cultural, ethnic and racial reconciliation in their congregations.

"George Yancey has written a remarkable book that makes a groundbreaking contribution. Drawing extensively on the first-ever national study of multiracial congregations, he uncovers seven main factors that these congregations have in common. He

takes us through these commonalities, step by step, in an engaging and easy-to-read manner. Contained in the book is the very heart of what it takes to transform one's church into a multiracial congregation, and what it takes to develop together once a church is demographically multiracial."

FROM THE FOREWORD BY MICHAEL O. EMERSON, FOUNDING DIRECTOR OF THE CENTER ON RACE, RELIGION AND URBAN LIFE, RICE UNIVERSITY; COAUTHOR OF *DIVIDED BY FAITH* AND *UNITED BY FAITH*

"Dr. Yancey has provided a helpful volume for the church as it takes on the globalization of our communities. Yancey's investigation has brought together numerous principles and illustrations on how best to develop the ministry of a multiethnic church.... He is deeply concerned that the multiethnic church not be an end in itself but a means to race reconciliation."

MANUEL ORTIZ, EMERITUS PROFESSOR OF PRACTICAL THEOLOGY, WESTMINSTER THEOLOGICAL SEMINARY; AUTHOR OF *ONE NEW PEOPLE*

***

George Yancey (Ph.D., University of Texas) is associate professor of sociology at the University of North

Texas, specializing in race/ethnicity and biracial families. He is the coauthor of *United by Faith* (Oxford), coeditor of *Just Don't Marry One* (Judson), and the author of *Beyond Black and White* (Baker) and *Beyond Racial Gridlock* (IVP Books). He is the founder of Reconciliation Consulting, helping churches and ministries develop and sustain a multiracial emphasis.

Books For ALL Kinds of Readers

At ReadHowYouWant we understand that one size does not fit all types of readers. Our innovative, patent pending technology allows us to design new formats to make reading easier and more enjoyable for you. This helps improve your speed of reading and your comprehension. Our EasyRead printed books have been optimized to improve word recognition, ease eye tracking by adjusting word and line spacing as well as minimizing hyphenation. Our EasyRead SuperLarge editions have been developed to make reading easier and more accessible for vision-impaired readers. We offer Braille and DAISY formats of our books and all popular E-Book formats.

We are continually introducing new formats based upon research and reader preferences. Visit our web-site to see all of our formats and learn how you can Personalize our books for yourself or as gifts. Sign up to Become A RHYW Registered Reader.

www.readhowyouwant.com

Printed in Great Britain
by Amazon